HOW TO DRAW
CARTOON CHARACTERS
FOR CREATIVE KIDS

ABOUT THE AUTHOR.
DAVID HAILWOOD HAS BEEN ACTIVE IN THE UK COMICS INDUSTRY FOR OVER 20 YEARS, CONTRIBUTING TO SUCH TITLES AS EGMONT'S BEST SELLING CHILDREN'S COMIC 'TOXIC', HOTCHPOTCH, AND 100% BIODEGRADABLE. HE HAS ALSO WORKED AS A SPECIAL SKILLS TUTOR, TEACHING FILM, ART, AND COMIC MAKING TECHNIQUES TO CHILDREN ACROSS THE SOUTH COAST OF ENGLAND.

www.davidhailwood.com

How To Draw Cartoon Characters For Creative Kids is published by Biomekazoik Press (biomekazoik@gmail.com).

With thanks to: Jenny Hailwood, Ian Kitt, Olivia Egbunike, Delapouite, Comicraft

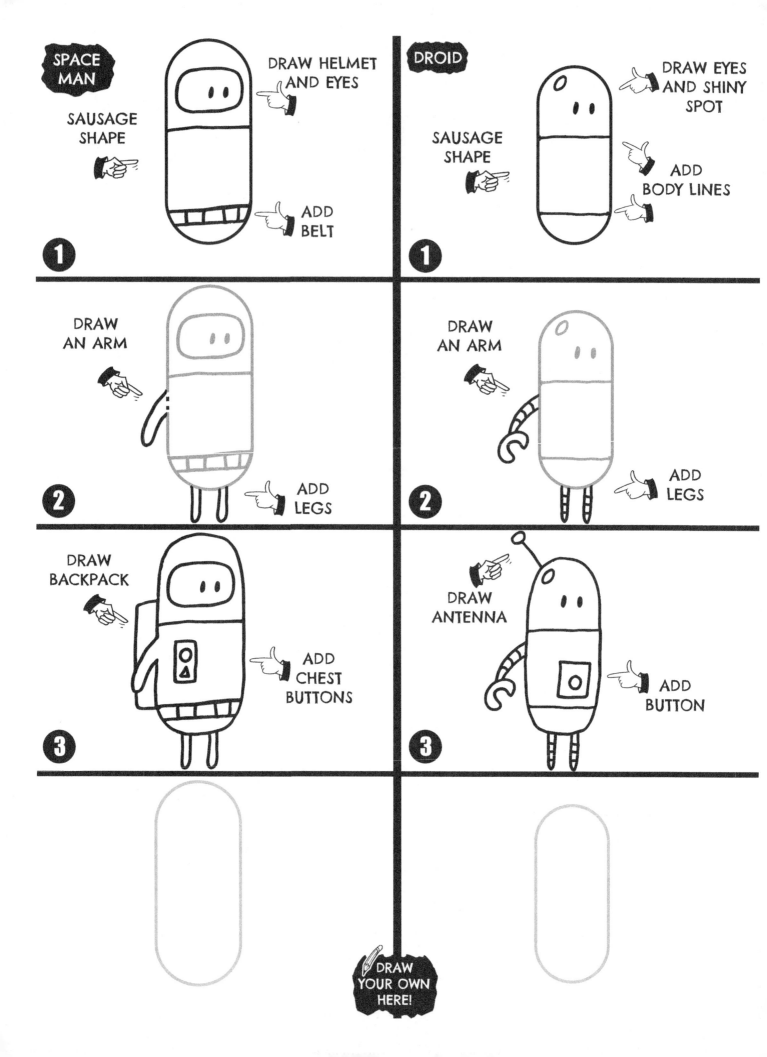

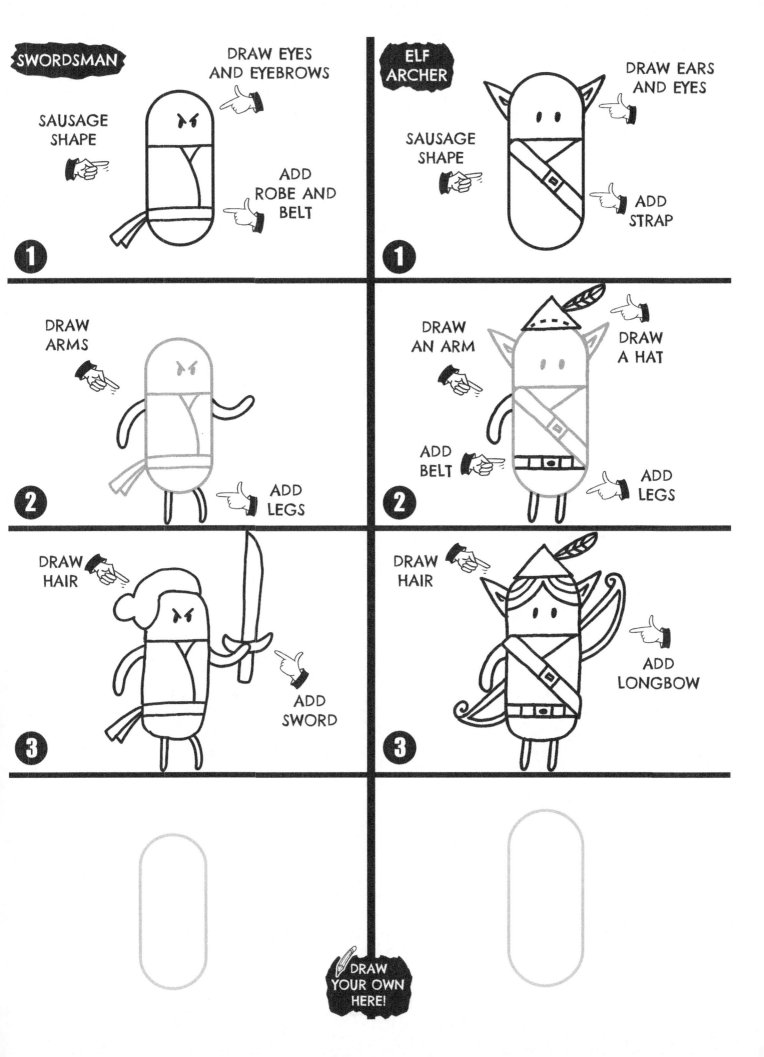

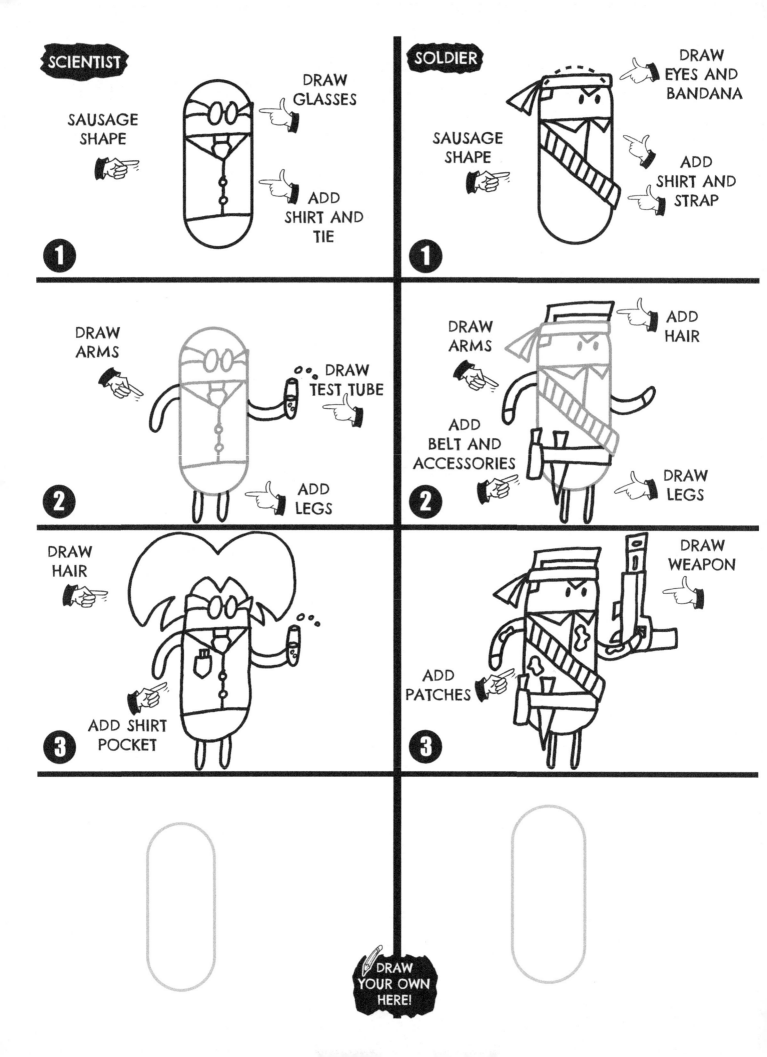

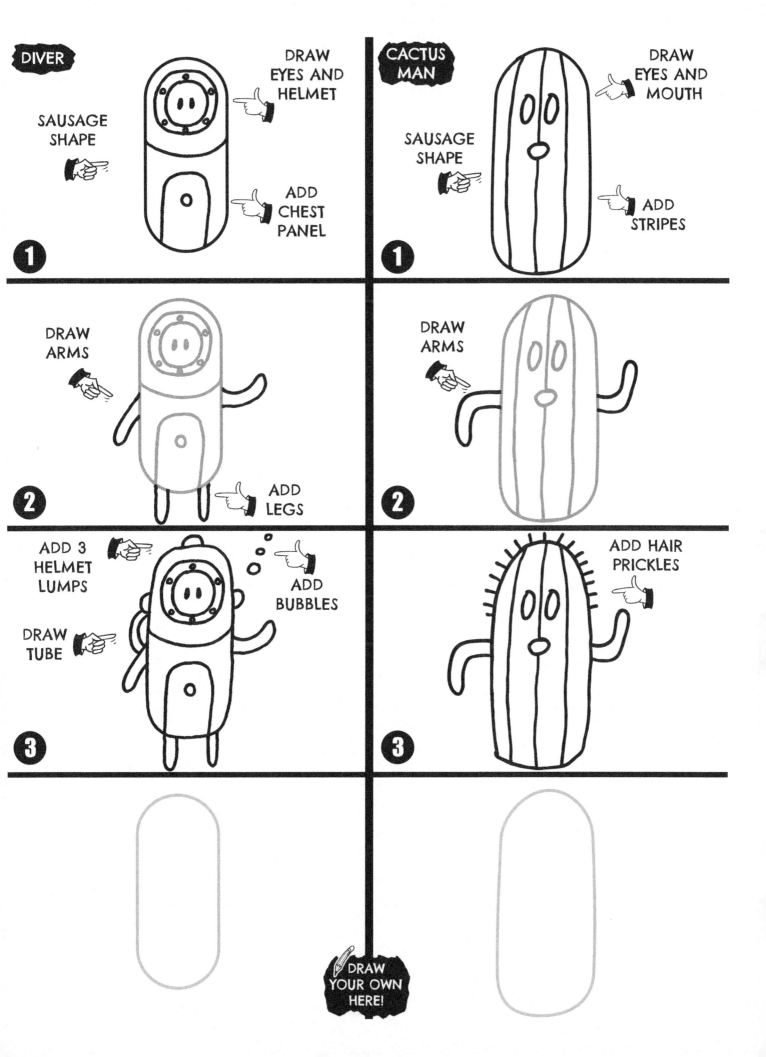

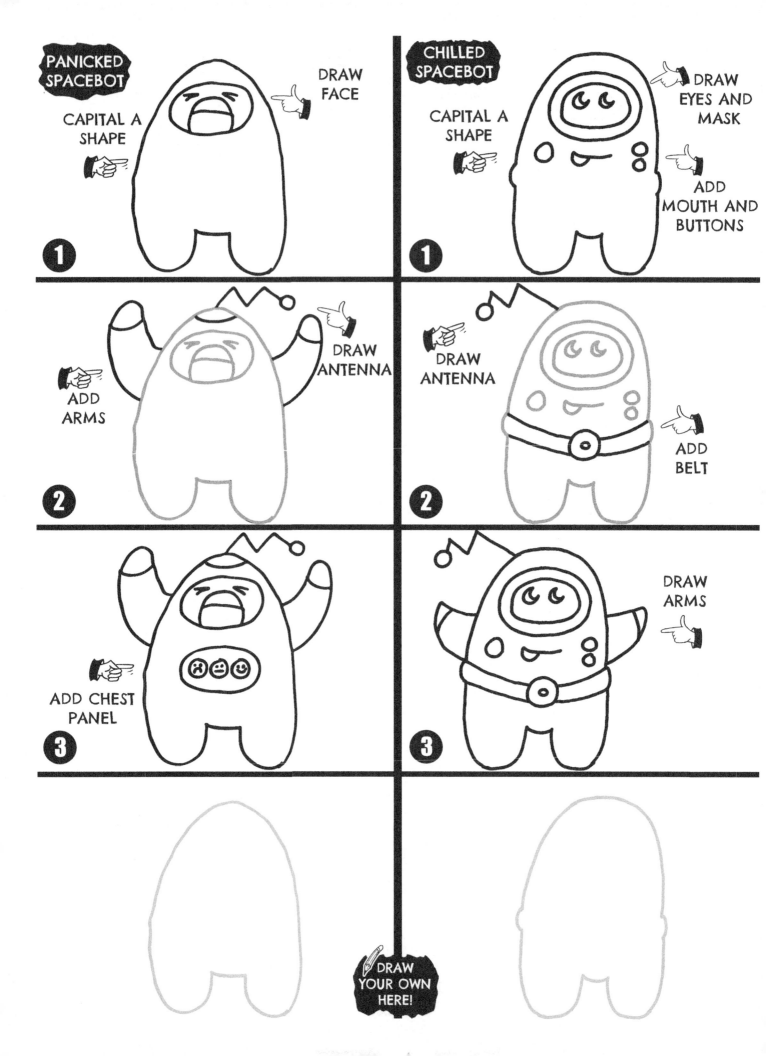

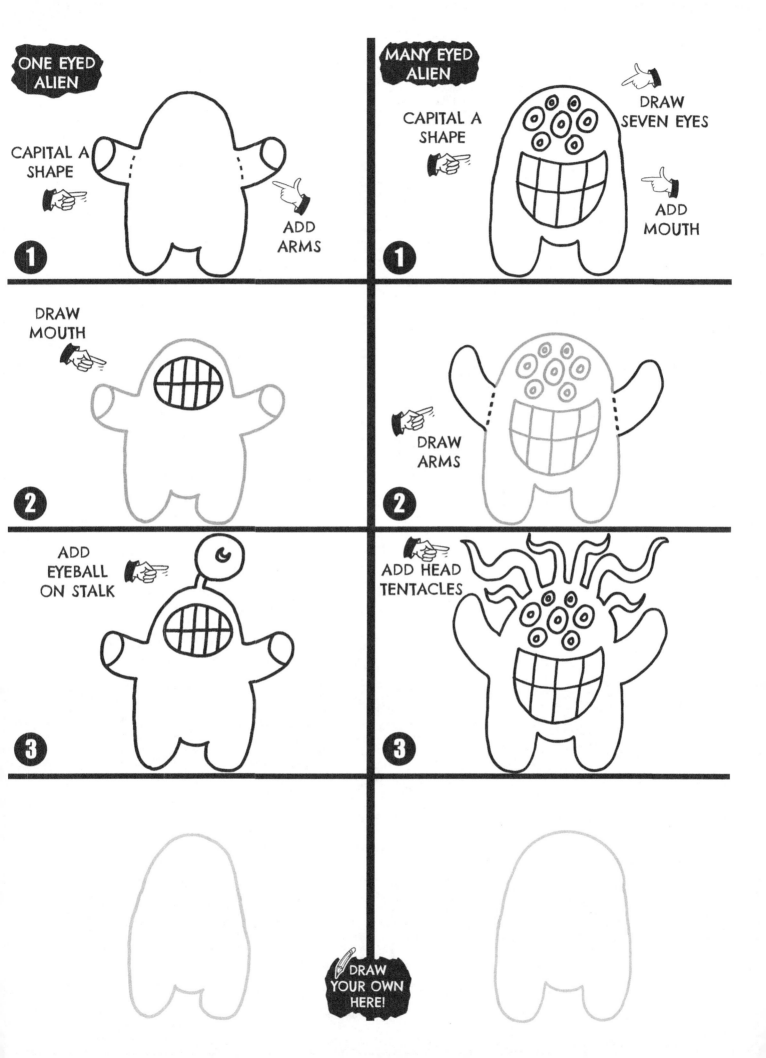

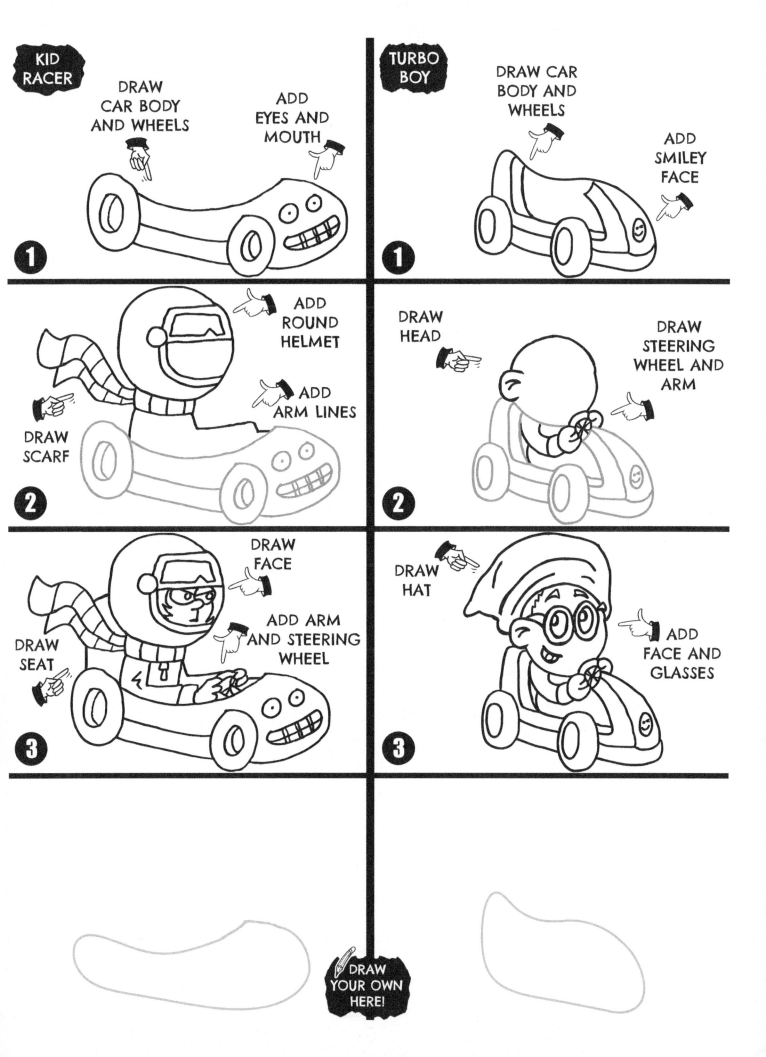

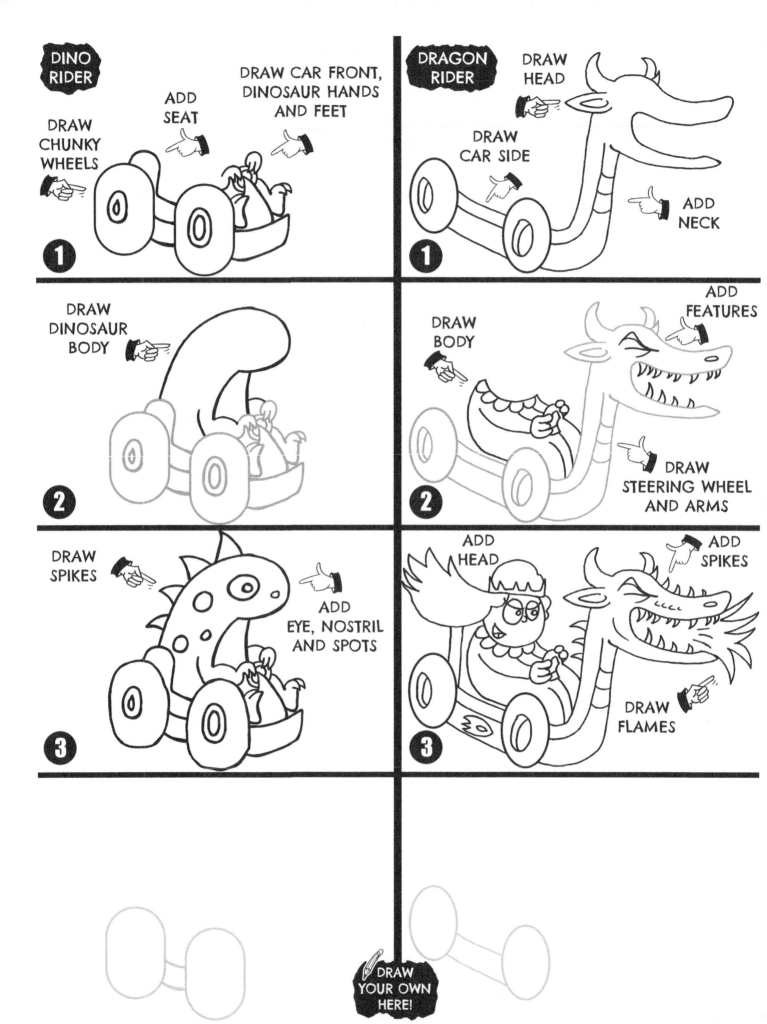

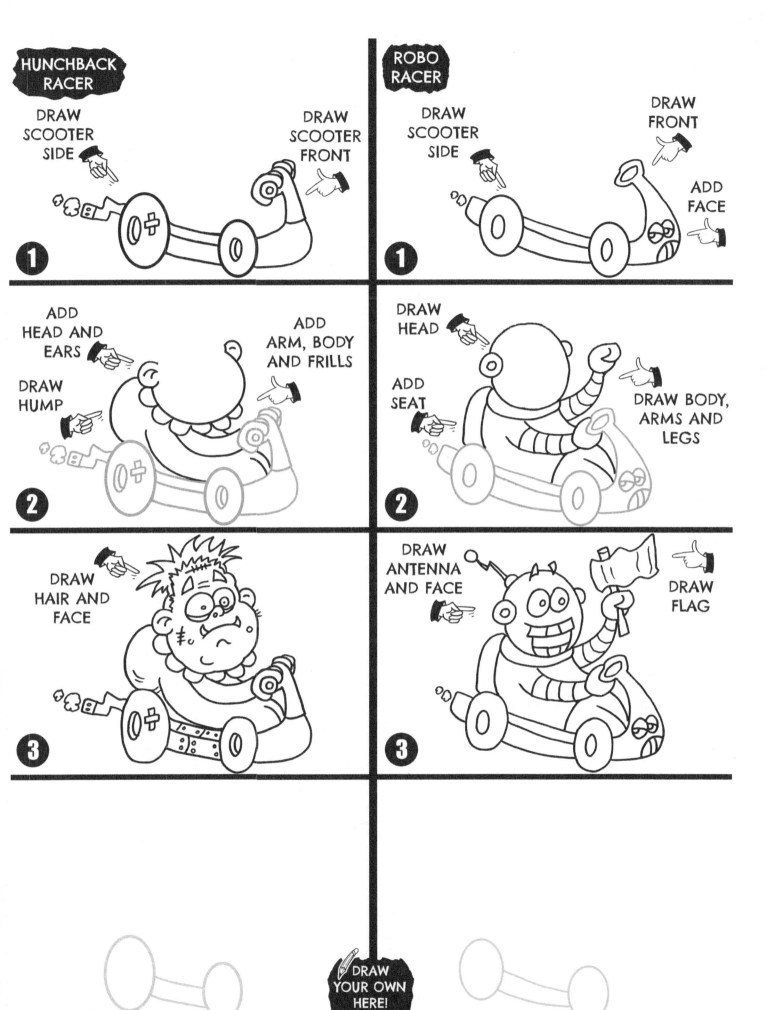

RACING KNIGHT

DRAW UNICORN HEAD

DRAW CAR SIDE

ADD NECK

1

ADD HELMET AND CLOAK

DRAW EYES AND REINS

ADD KNIGHTS ARM AND FOOT

2

DRAW PLUME AND VISOR

ADD MANE

3

WIZARD RACER

DRAW CAR SIDE

ADD CAR FRONT, WIZARD HANDS AND FEET

1

DRAW BEARD AND MOUTH

ADD BODY AND ARM

2

ADD HAT AND HAIR

DRAW EYES, NOSE AND EYEBROWS

ADD STAR TRAIL

3

DRAW YOUR OWN HERE!

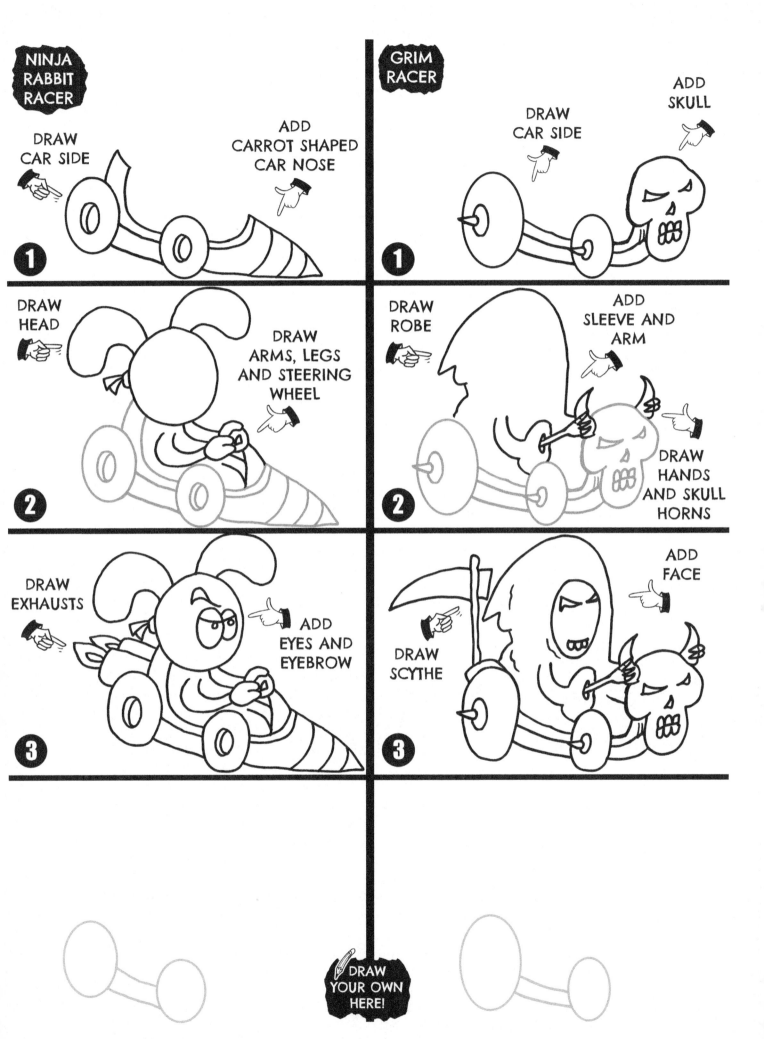

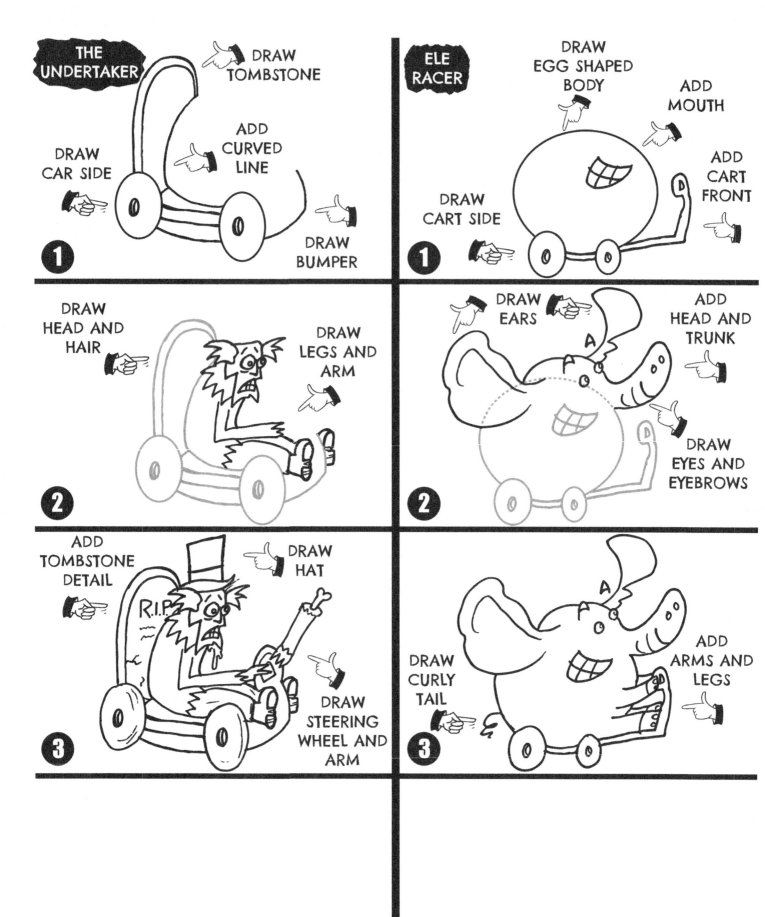

THE UNDERTAKER

1 DRAW CAR SIDE · ADD CURVED LINE · DRAW TOMBSTONE · DRAW BUMPER

2 DRAW HEAD AND HAIR · DRAW LEGS AND ARM

3 ADD TOMBSTONE DETAIL · DRAW HAT · DRAW STEERING WHEEL AND ARM · R.I.P.

ELE RACER

1 DRAW CART SIDE · DRAW EGG SHAPED BODY · ADD MOUTH · ADD CART FRONT

2 DRAW EARS · ADD HEAD AND TRUNK · DRAW EYES AND EYEBROWS

3 DRAW CURLY TAIL · ADD ARMS AND LEGS

DRAW YOUR OWN HERE!

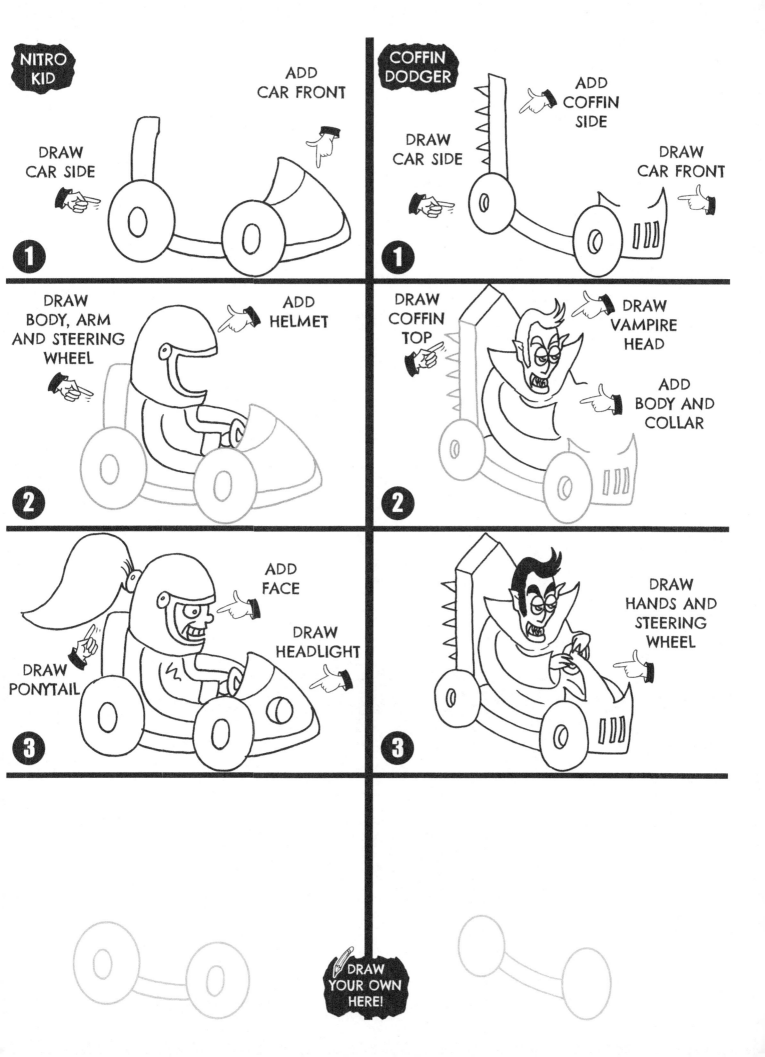

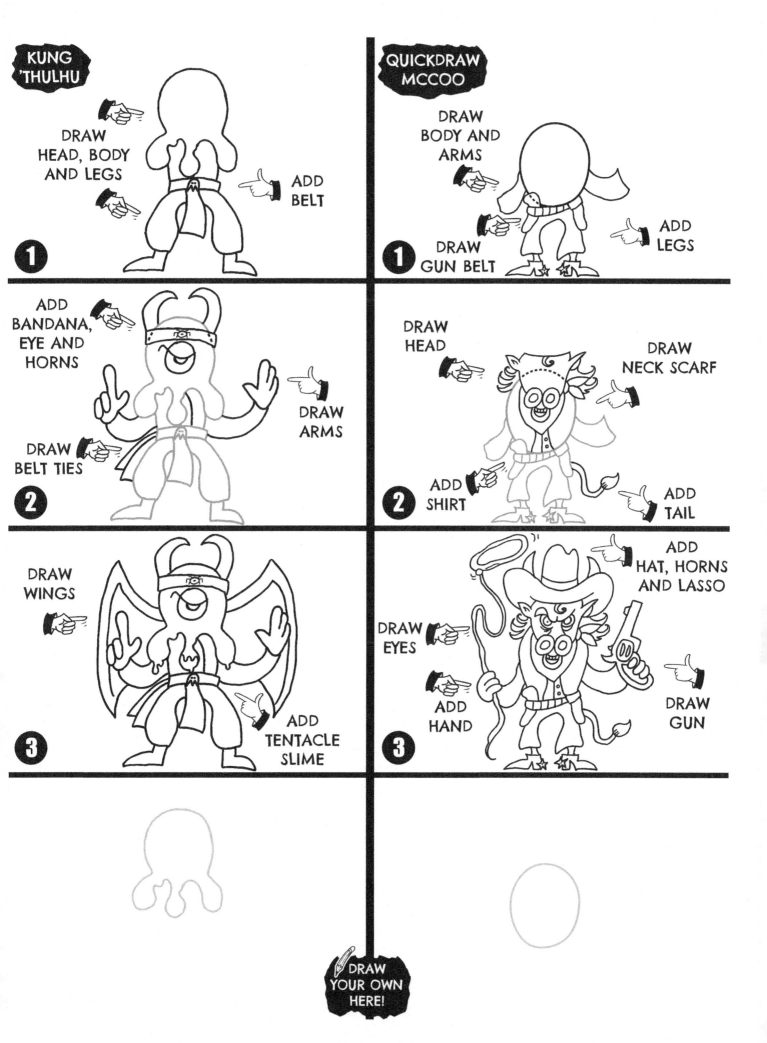

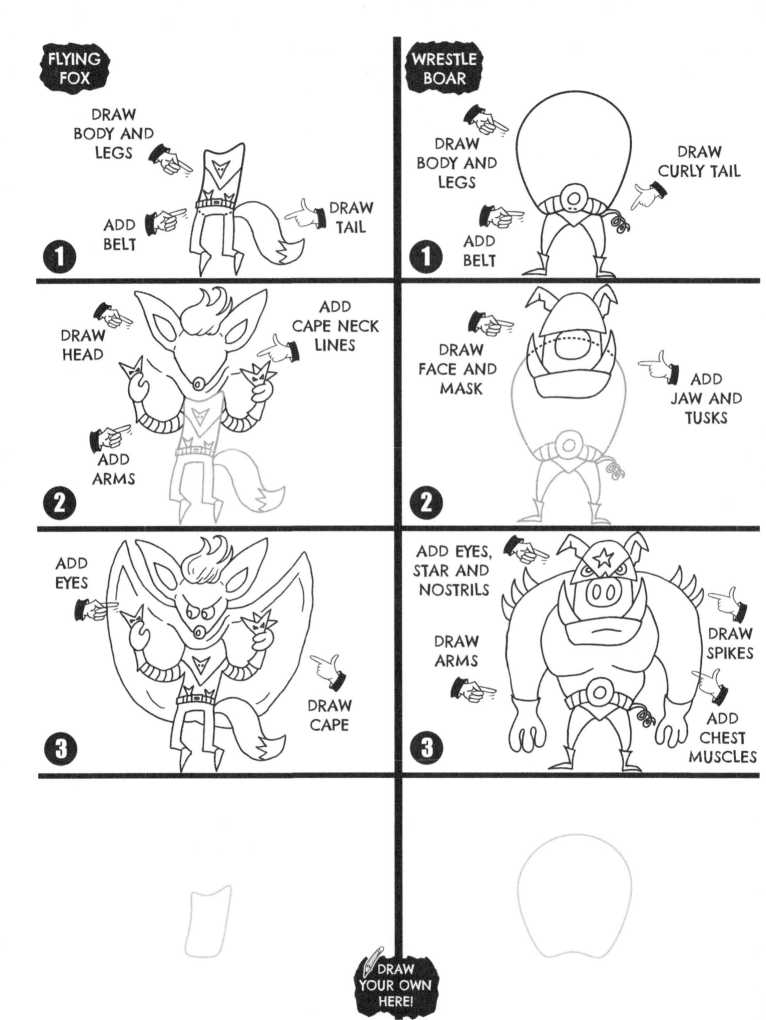

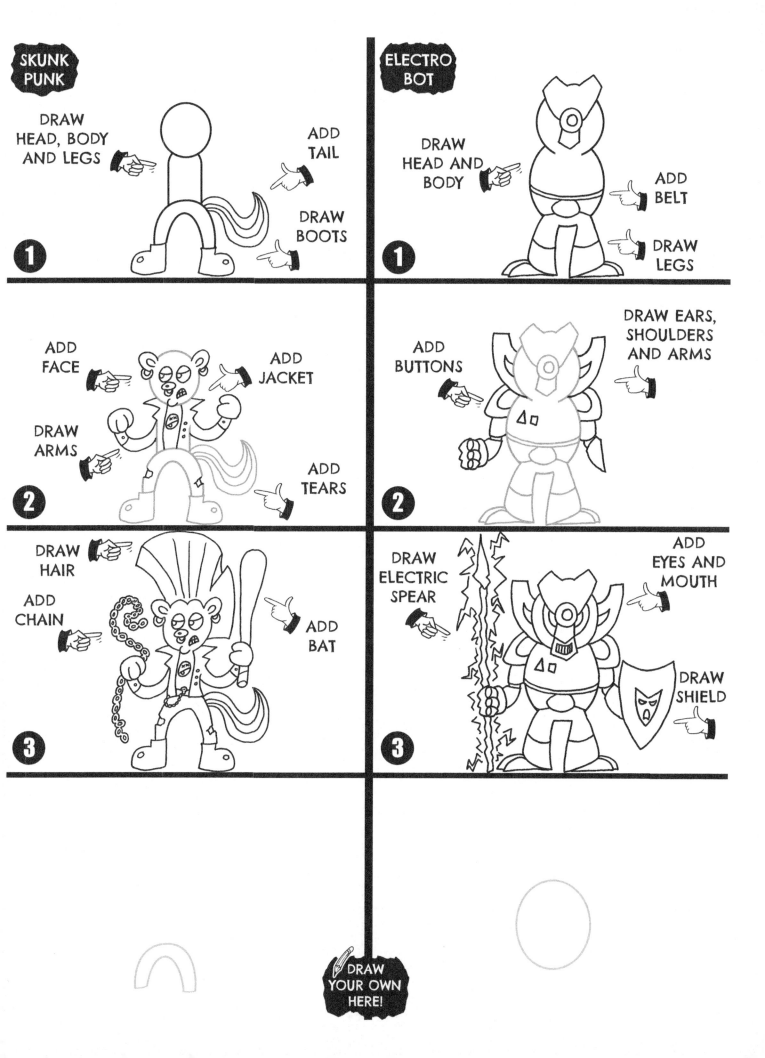

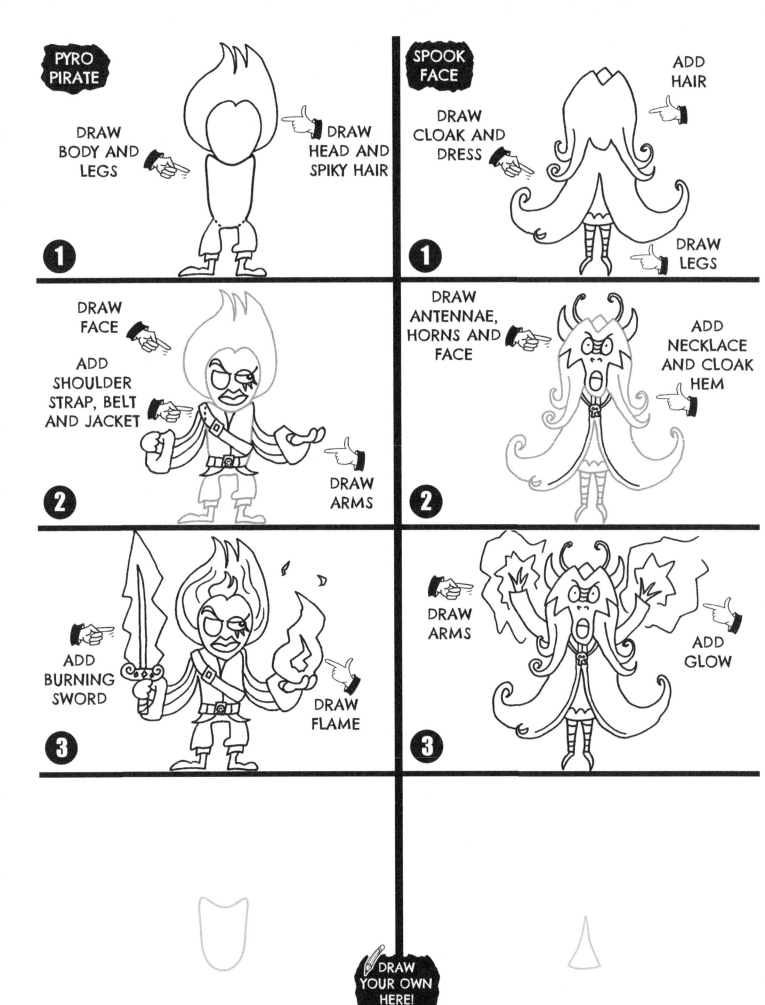

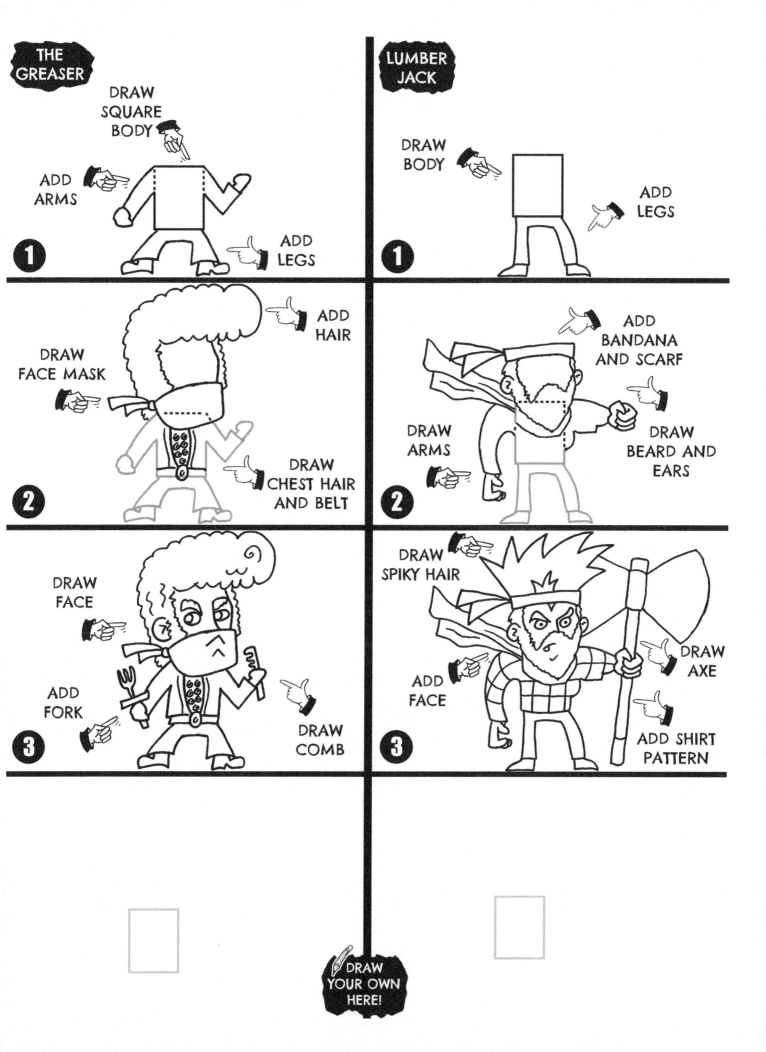

ROLE PLAYING GAME HEROES

WITCH HUNTER

1 — ADD HAT AND HAIR · DRAW COLLAR (W SHAPE) · DRAW BODY

2 — DRAW HAT BUCKLE · ADD FACE · DRAW COAT CREASE AND BUTTONS

3 — ADD CROSSBOW · DRAW HAND

RONIN

1 — DRAW HAT · DRAW BODY · ADD BELT

2 — DRAW TOPKNOT · ADD ARM · DRAW ARM AND SWORD

3 — DRAW EYES AND MOUTH · ADD DETAIL TO ROBE AND HAT

DRAW YOUR OWN HERE!

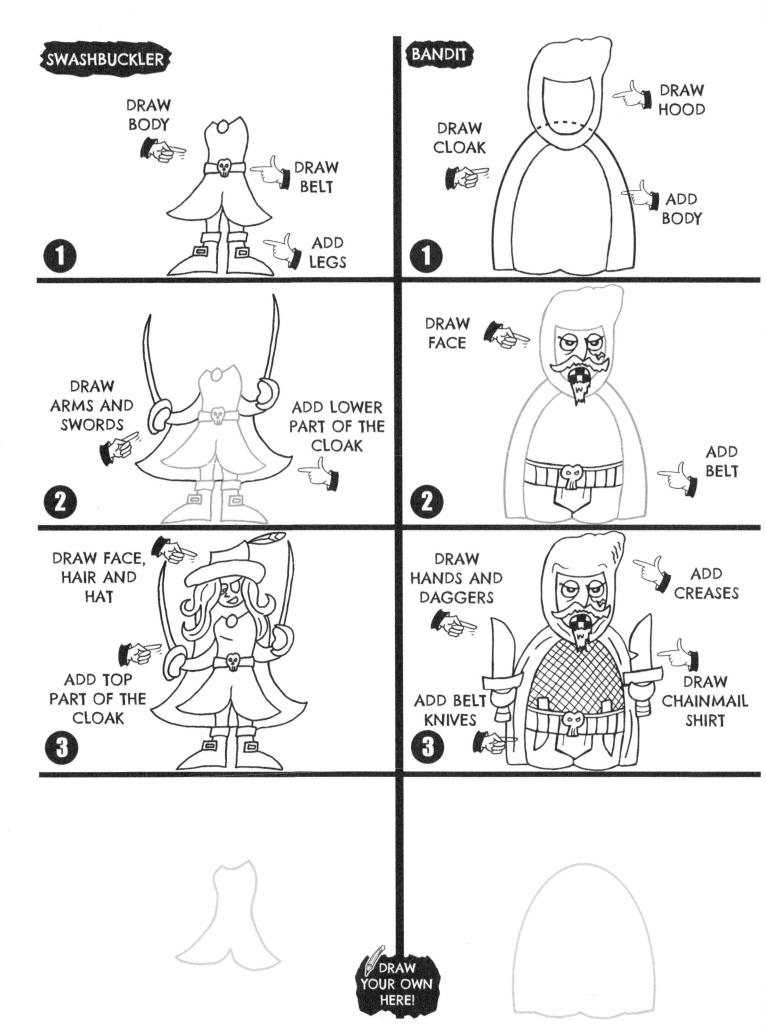

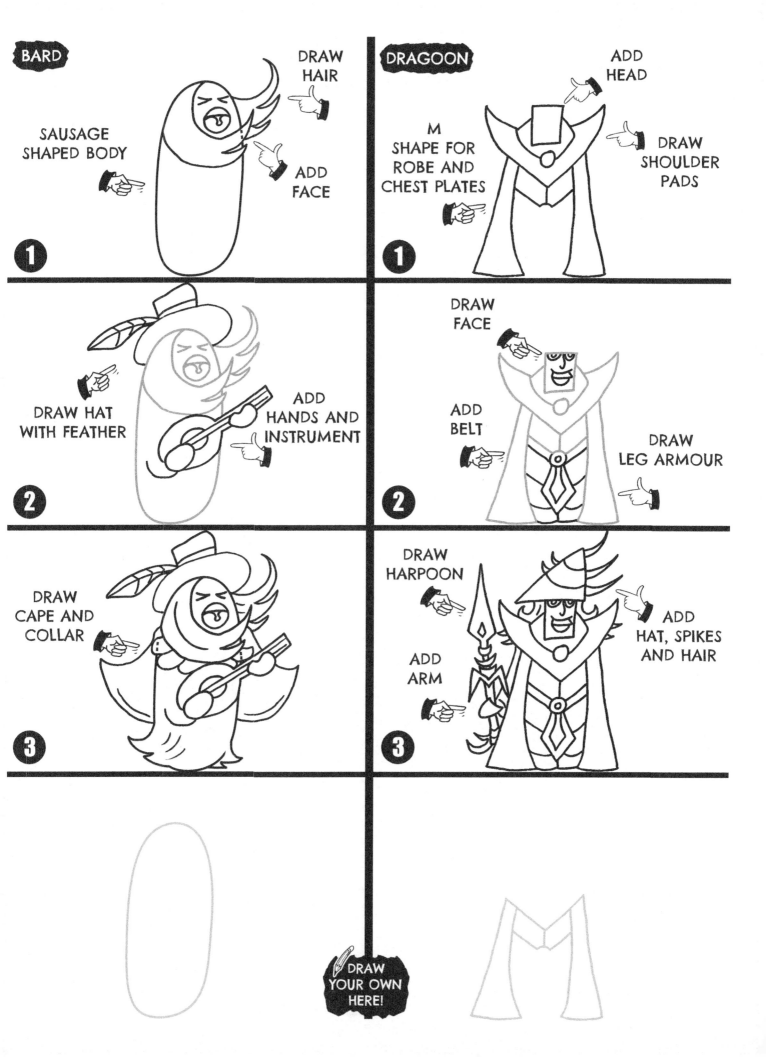

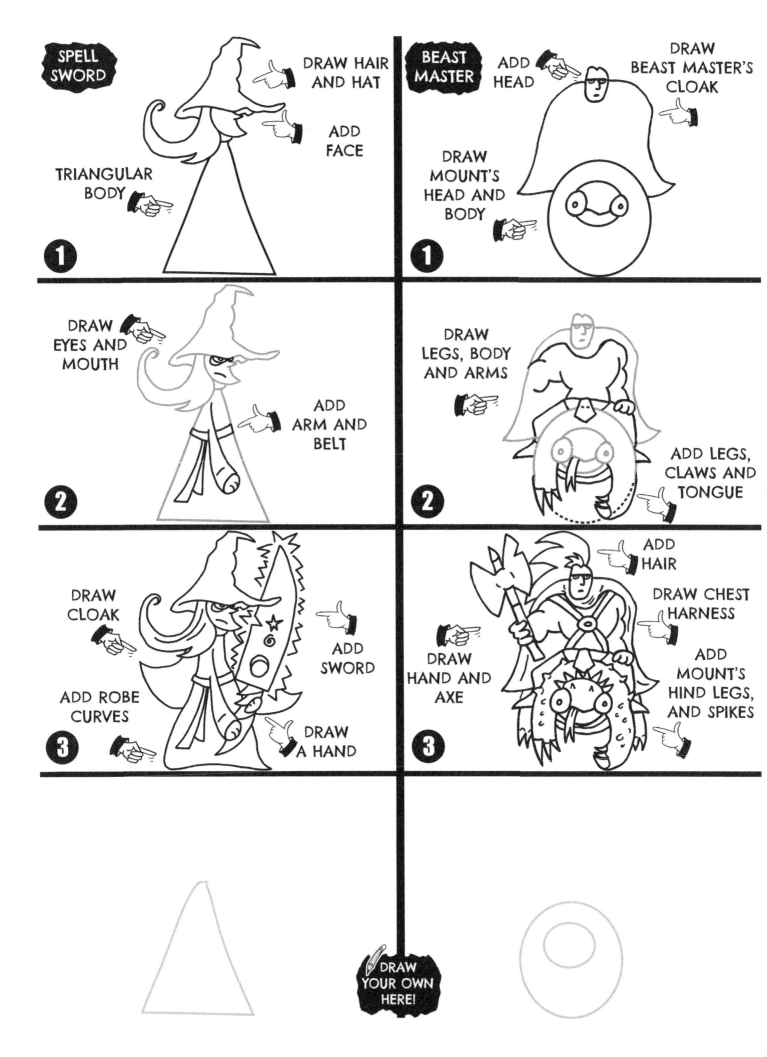

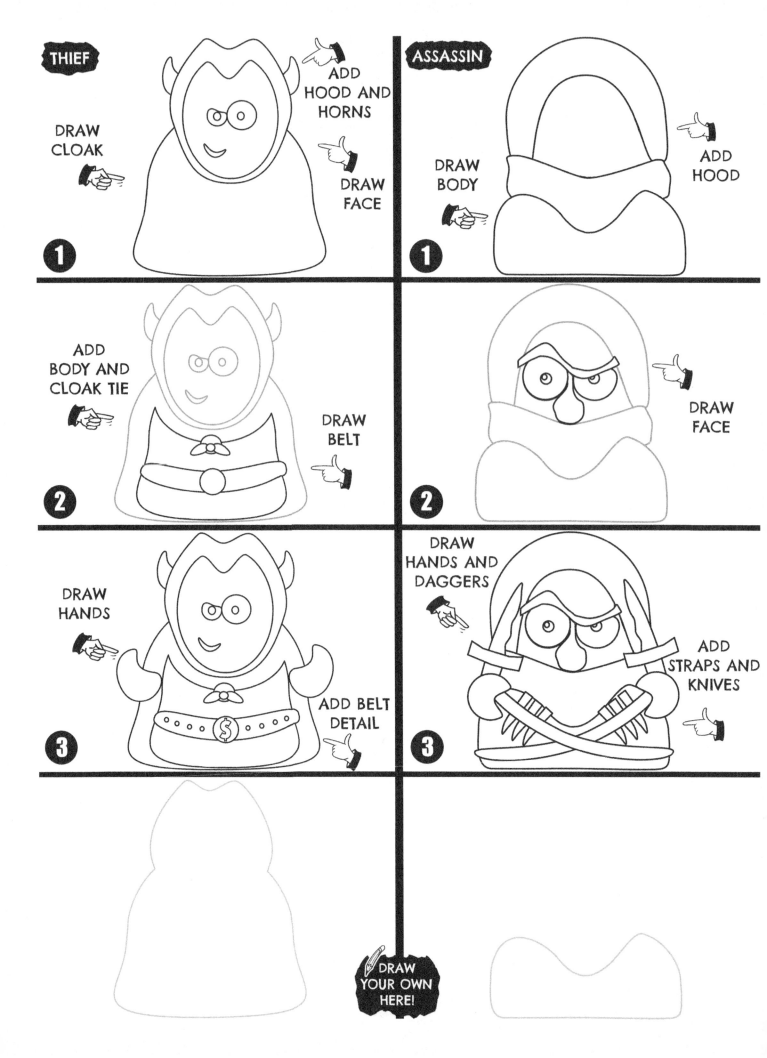

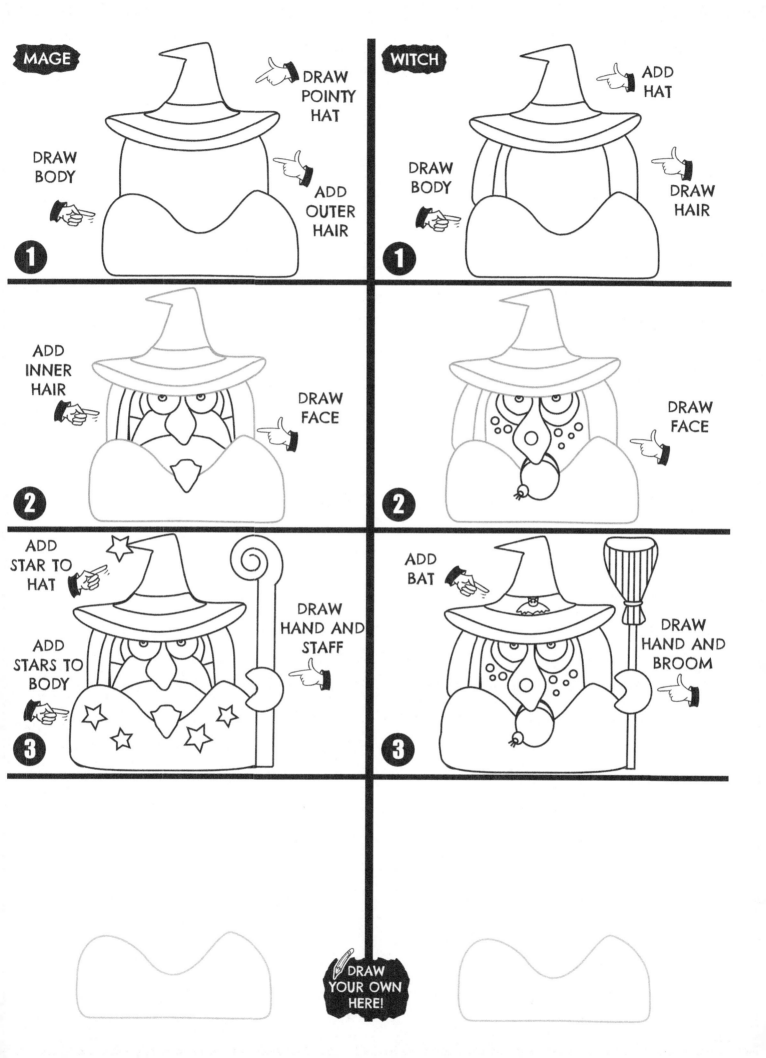

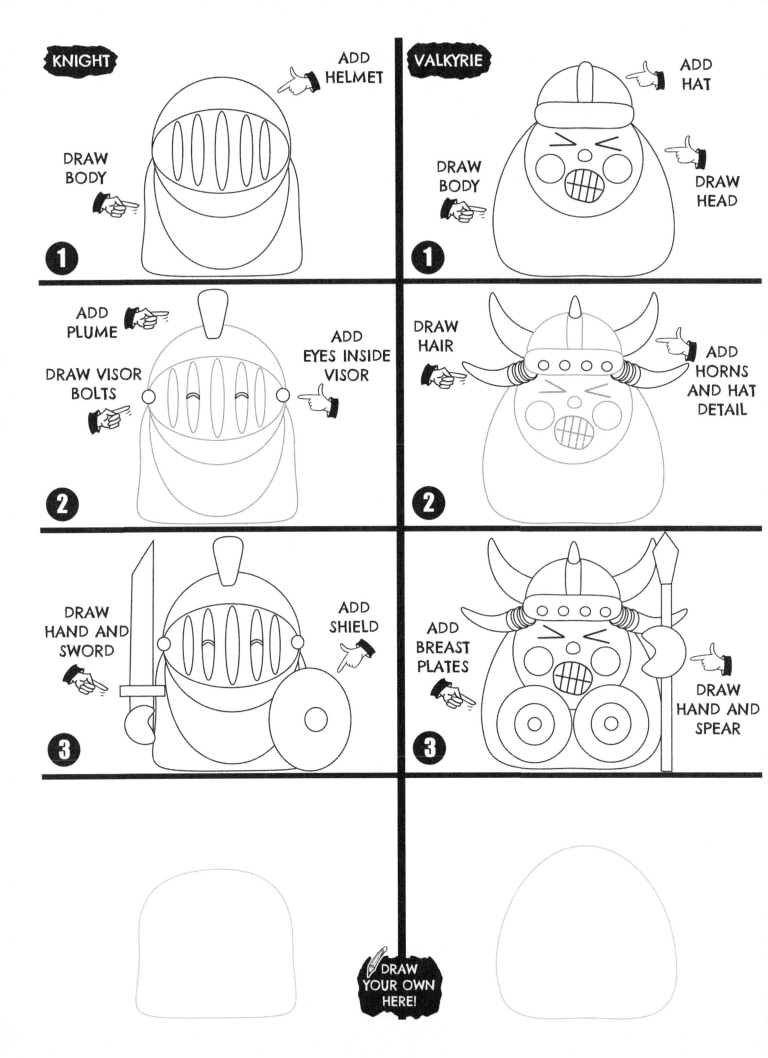

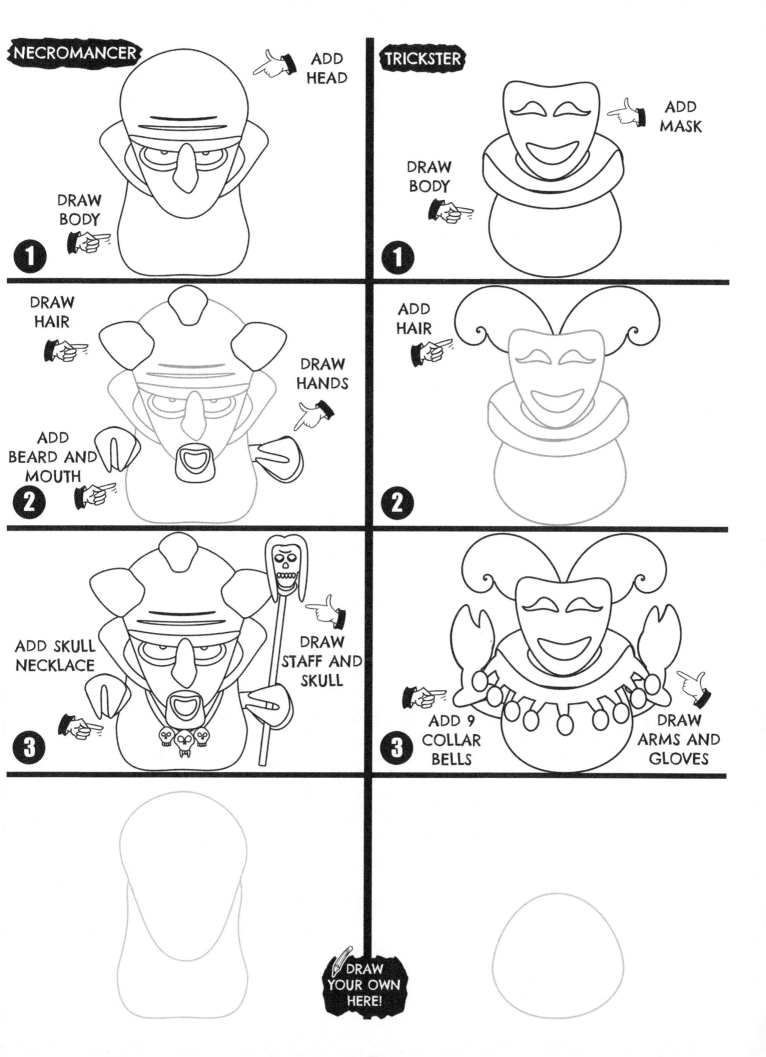

ROLE PLAYING GAME MONSTERS

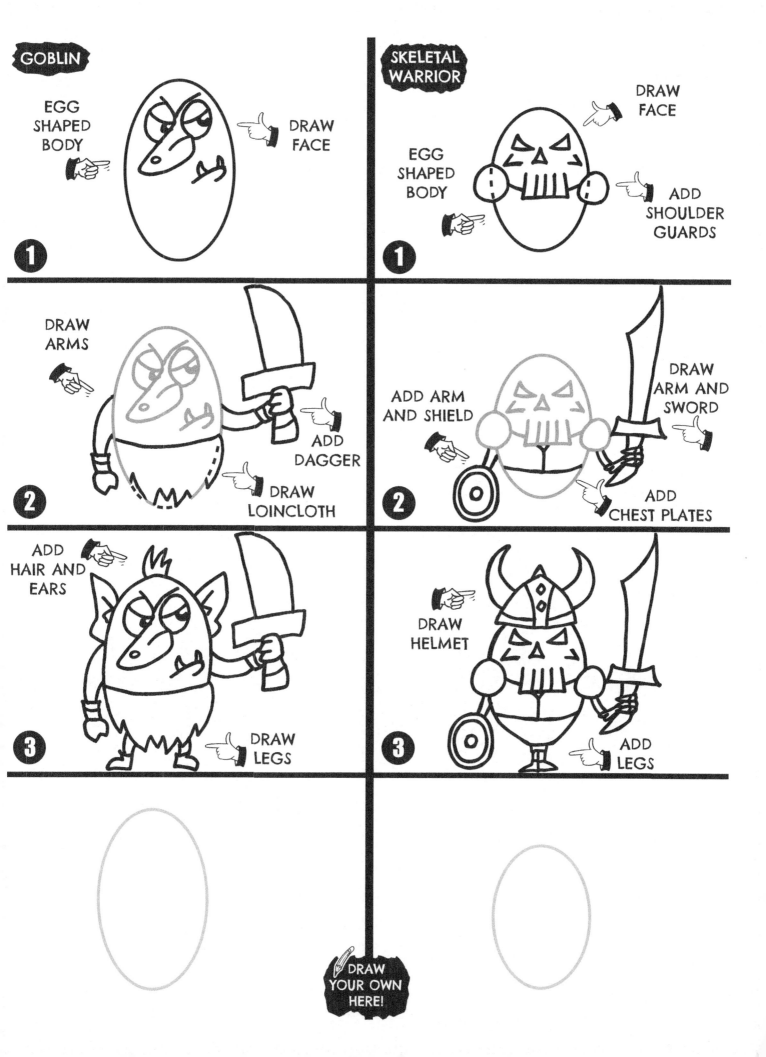

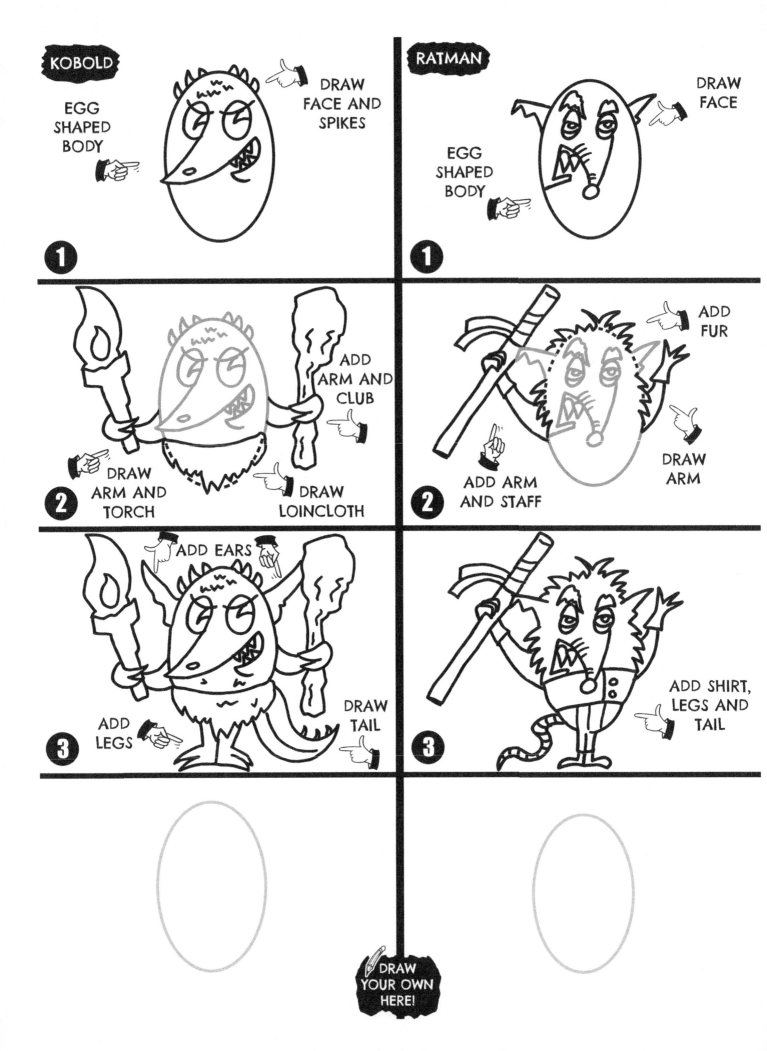

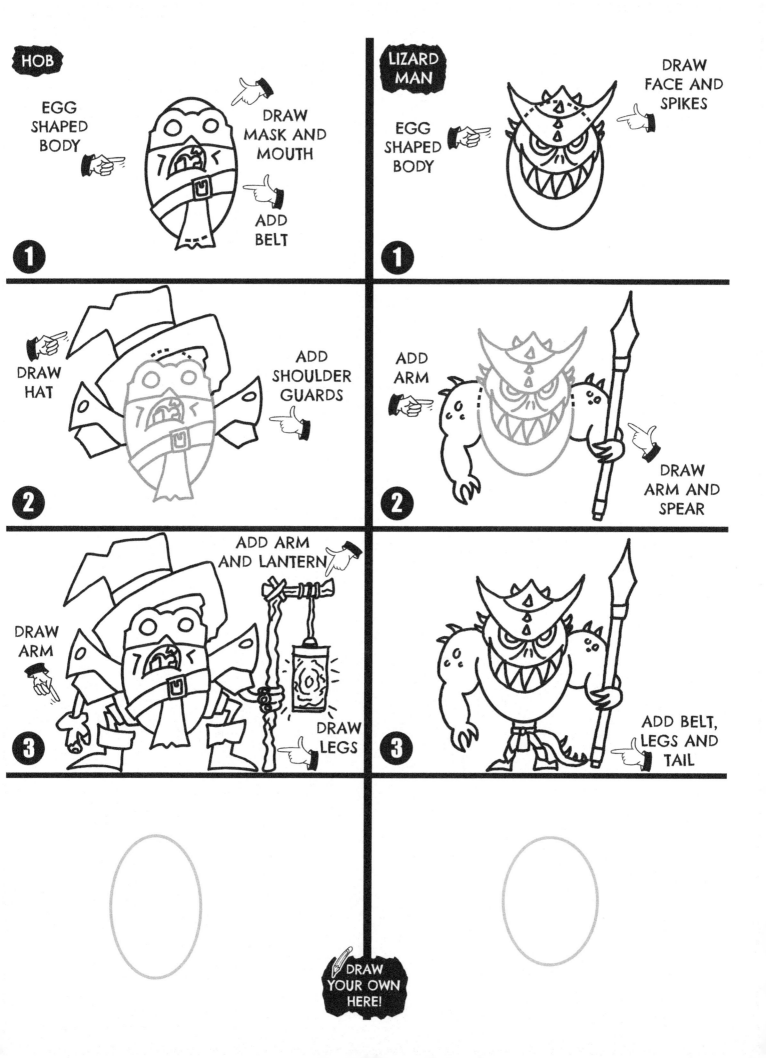

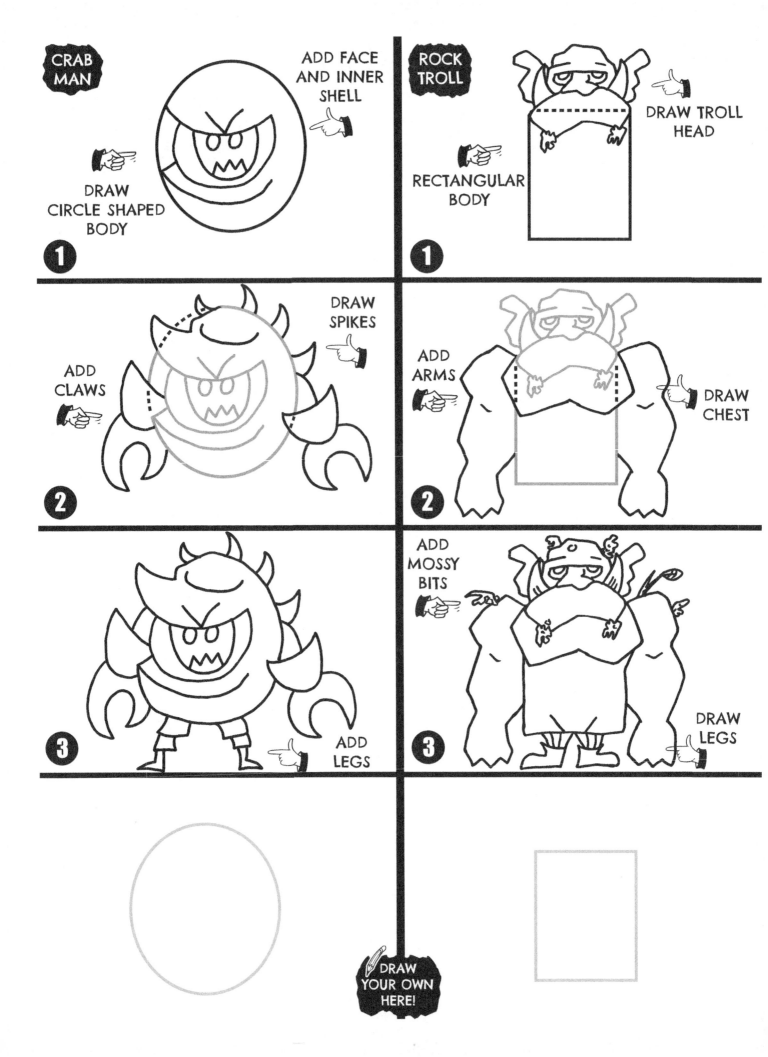

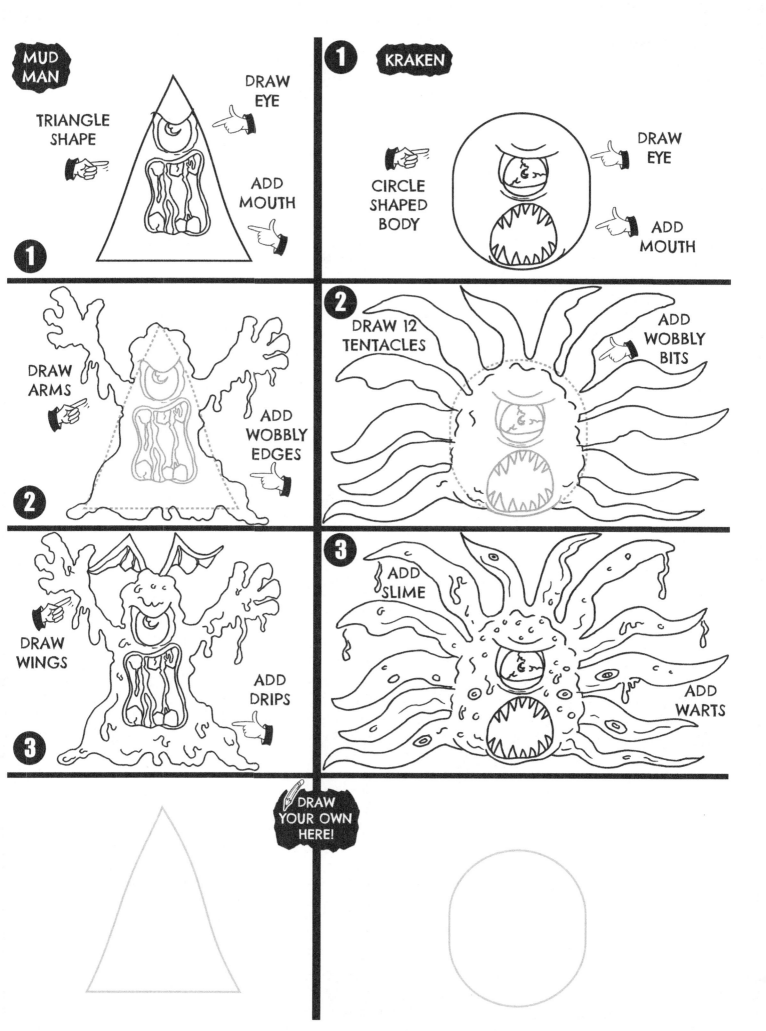

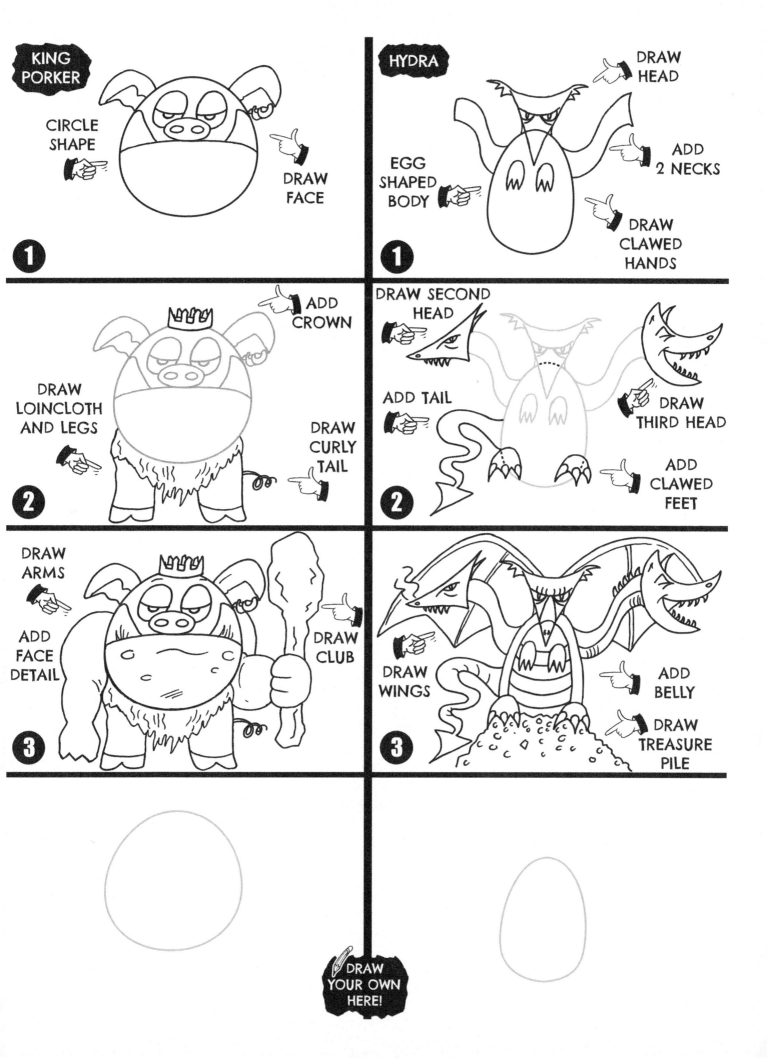

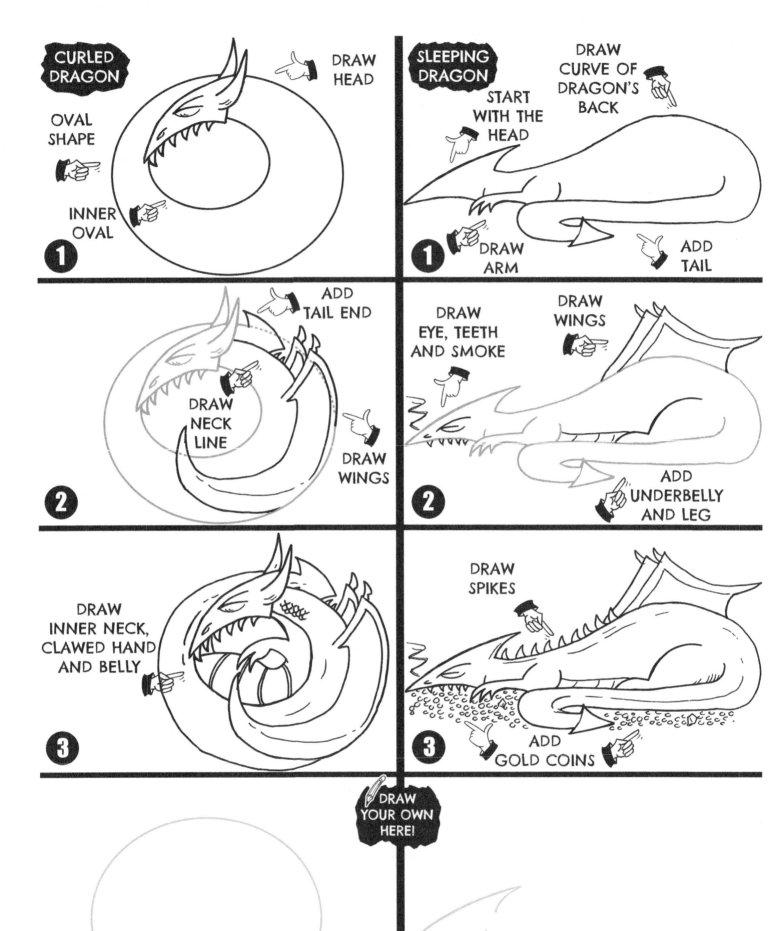

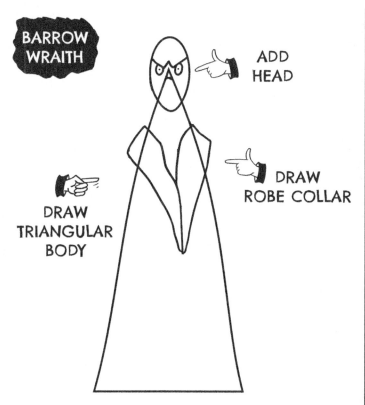

ADD HEAD

DRAW ROBE COLLAR

DRAW TRIANGULAR BODY

1

DRAW CROWN

ADD HAIR

DRAW ROBE ARMS

ADD HANDS

2

DRAW FACE

ADD HAIR DETAIL

ADD GLOW

ADD BELT AND DAGGER

ADD ROBE CURLS

3

DRAW YOUR OWN HERE!

FARMING

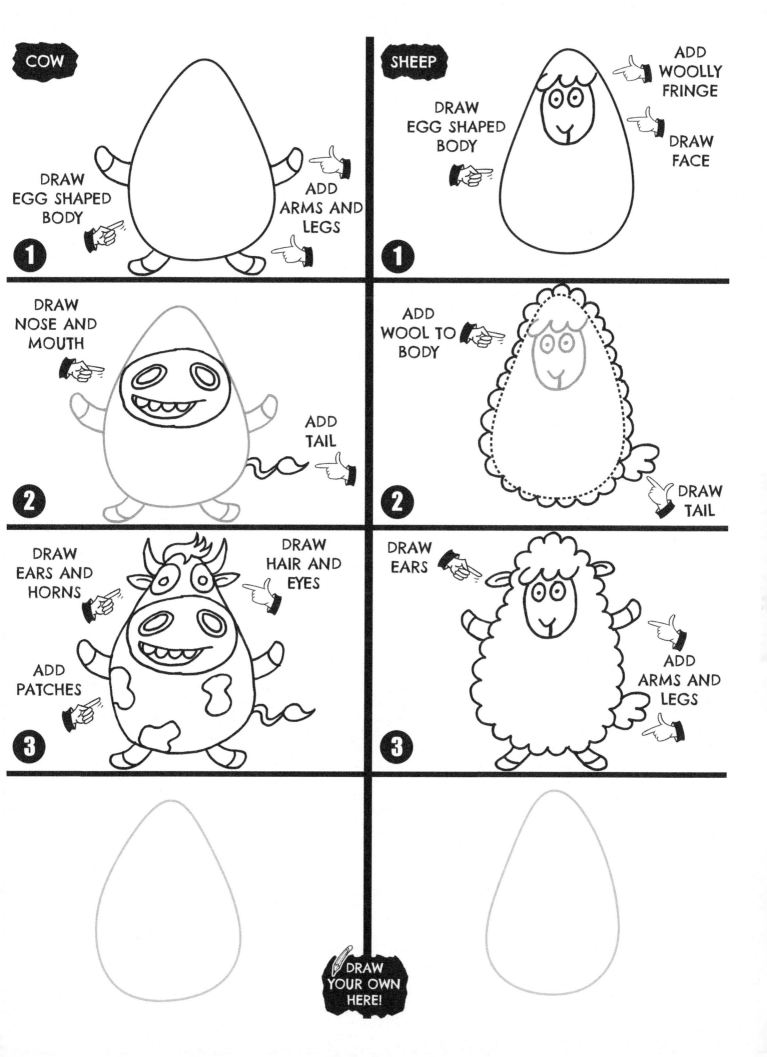

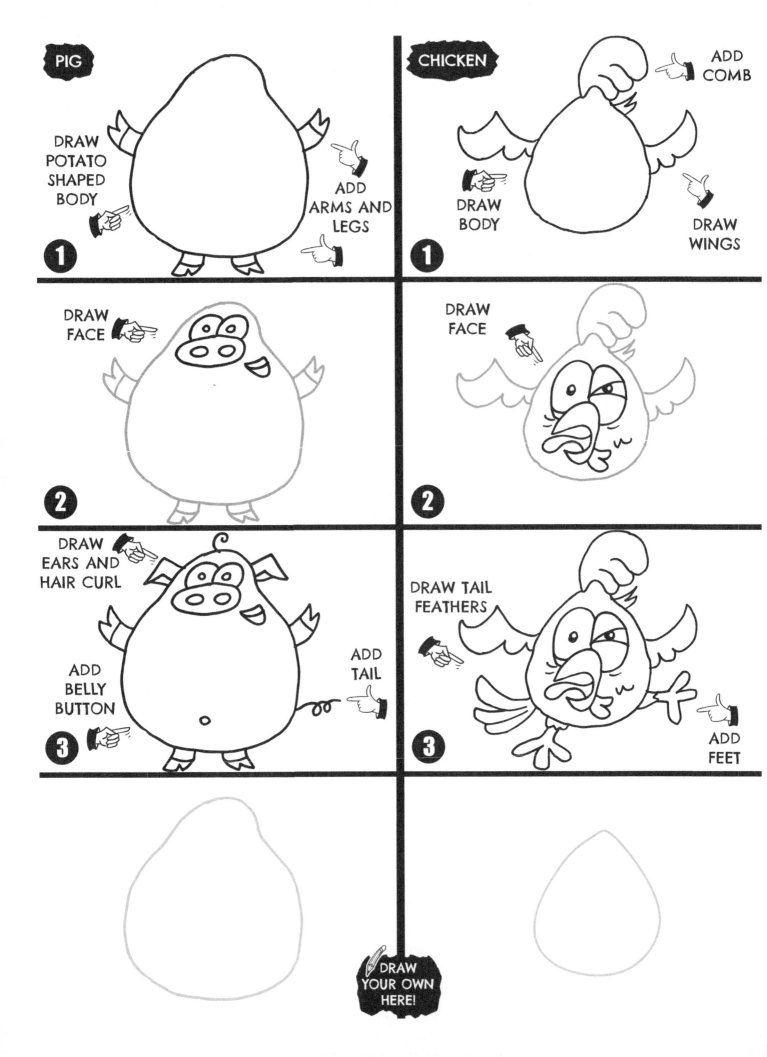

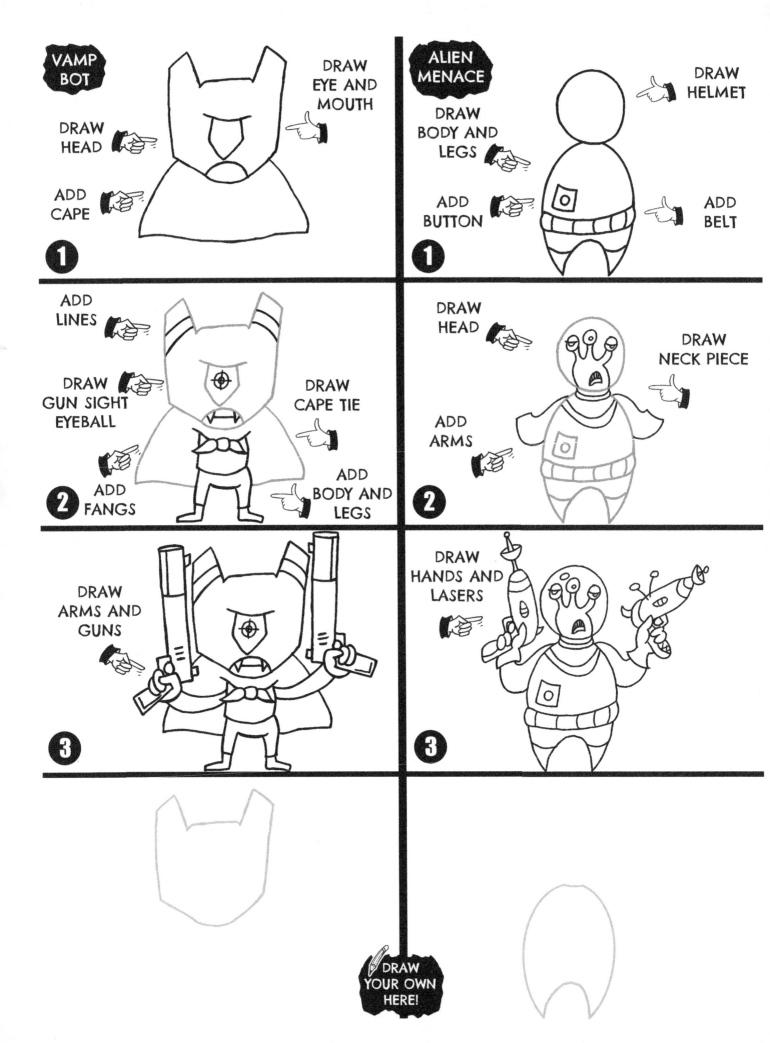

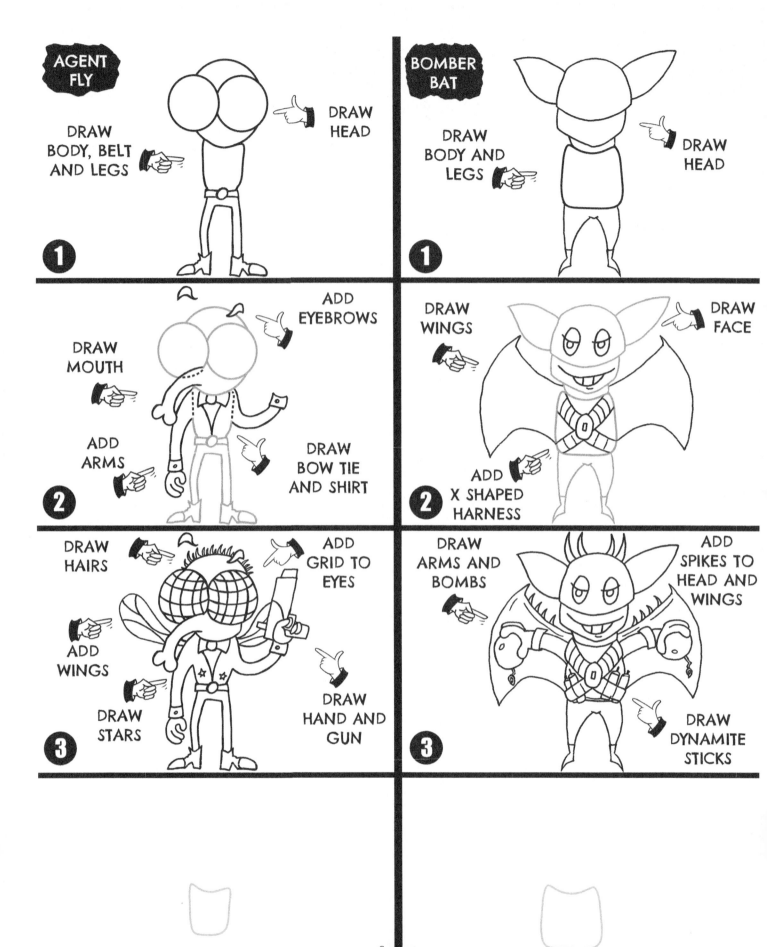

AGENT FLY

1. DRAW BODY, BELT AND LEGS
   DRAW HEAD

2. ADD EYEBROWS
   DRAW MOUTH
   ADD ARMS
   DRAW BOW TIE AND SHIRT

3. DRAW HAIRS
   ADD GRID TO EYES
   ADD WINGS
   DRAW STARS
   DRAW HAND AND GUN

BOMBER BAT

1. DRAW BODY AND LEGS
   DRAW HEAD

2. DRAW WINGS
   DRAW FACE
   ADD X SHAPED HARNESS

3. DRAW ARMS AND BOMBS
   ADD SPIKES TO HEAD AND WINGS
   DRAW DYNAMITE STICKS

DRAW YOUR OWN HERE!

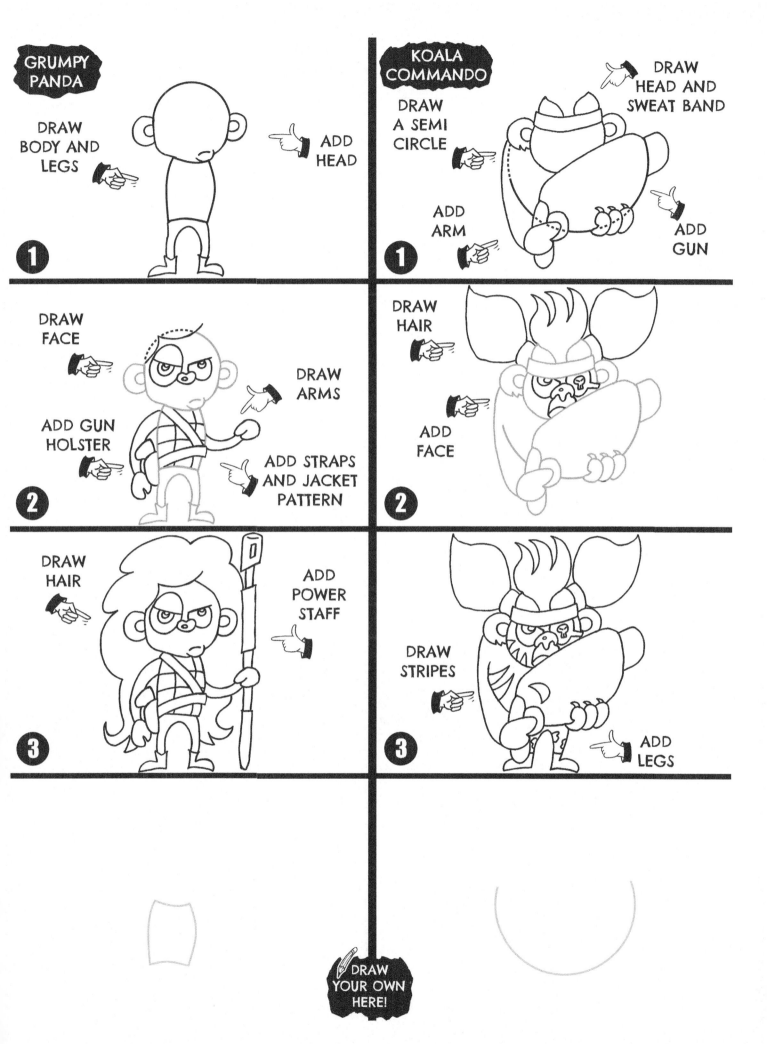

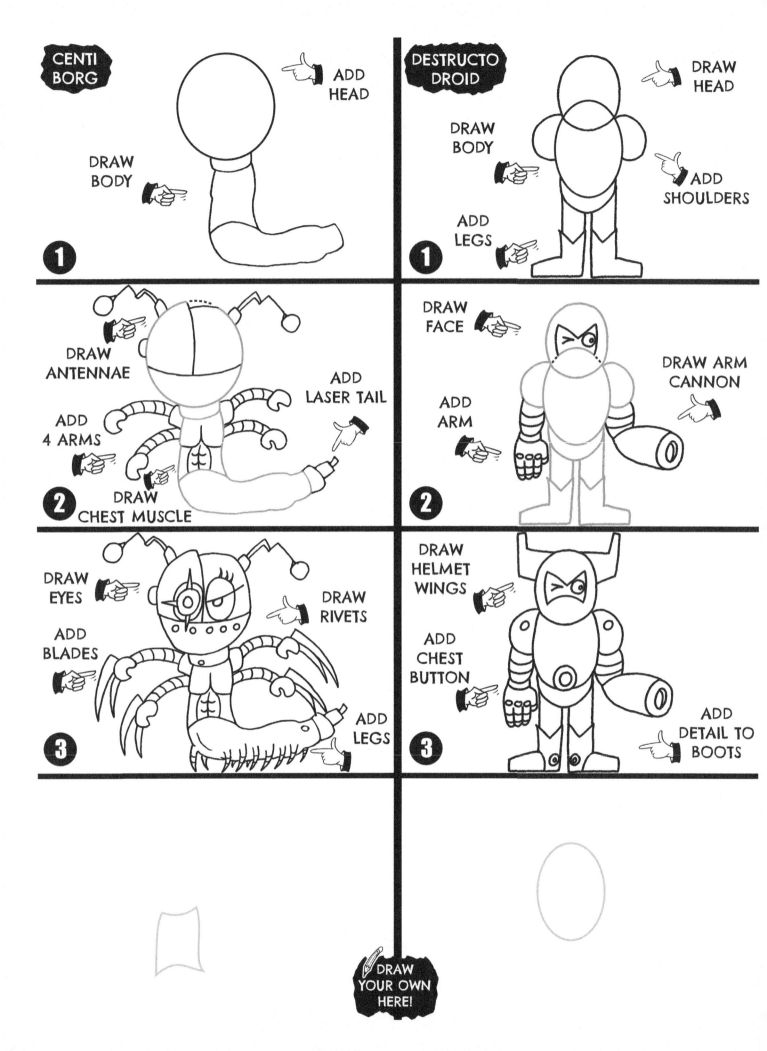

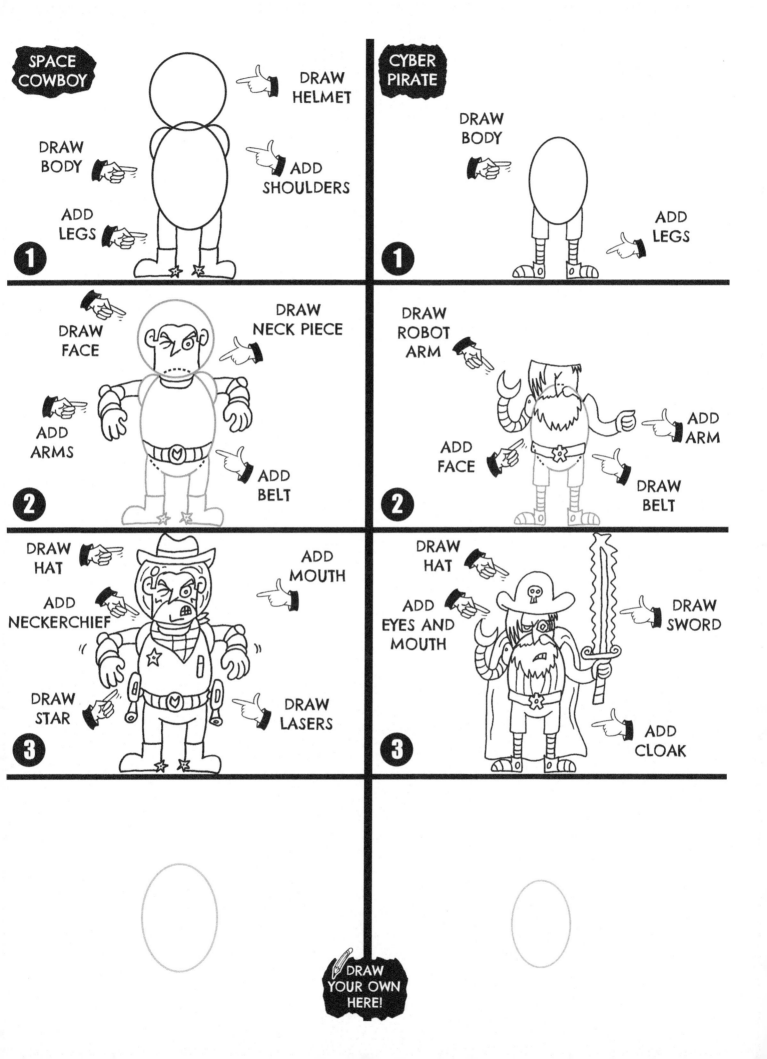

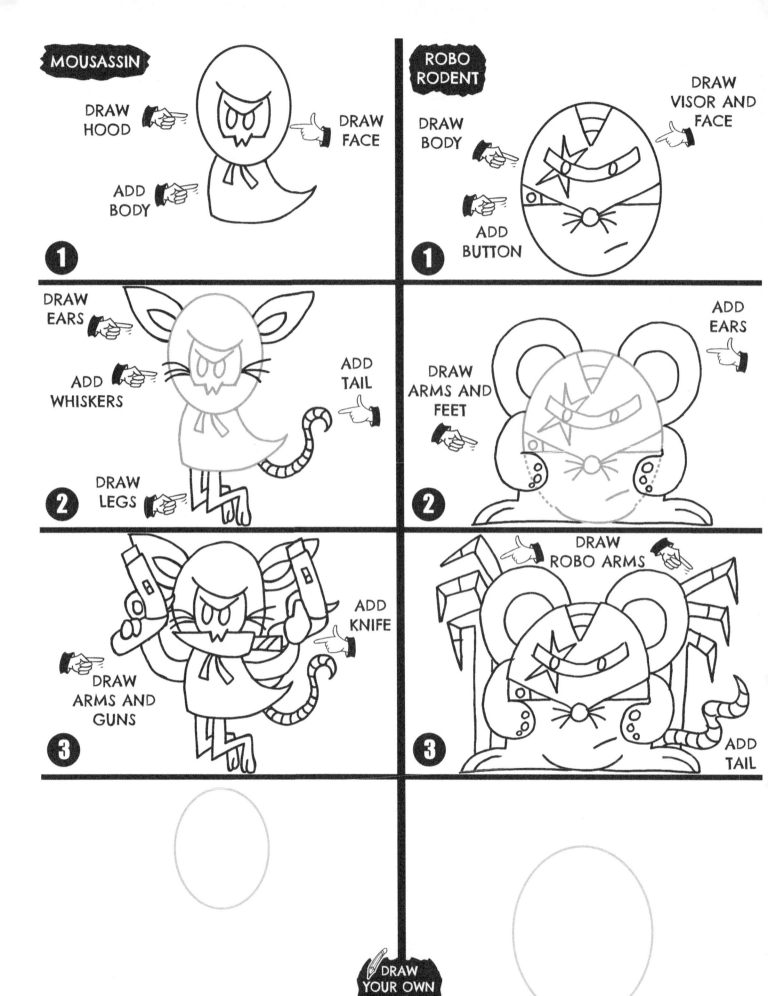

GREETINGS, AND WELCOME TO THE COMIC CREATION SECTION - OVERFLOWING WITH EMPTY COMIC PANELS JUST WAITING TO BE FILLED!

WHEN CREATING A COMIC THE ONLY LIMIT IS YOUR IMAGINATION.

EITHER CREATE YOUR VERY OWN CHARACTERS TO USE IN YOUR COMIC, OR USE THE ONES PROVIDED IN THE FIRST SECTION.

BUT FIRST, A FEW TIPS.

WHEN A CHARACTER IN A COMIC SPEAKS, THEIR WORDS GO INSIDE A **SPEECH BALLOON** LIKE THIS ONE.

THE **TAIL** OF THE BALLOON ALWAYS POINTS TOWARDS THE CHARACTER'S **MOUTH**.

BALLOON TAIL.

MEANWHILE, IN A WELL CONCEALED SPACESHIP JUST ABOVE EARTH...

GURRRGLE! **CAPTION BOXES** LIKE THE ONE ABOVE CAN BE USED TO GIVE READERS **IMPORTANT INFORMATION**, SUCH AS A CHANGE OF LOCATION BETWEEN PANELS.

GURRRGLE!

DON'T FORGET TO THROW IN SOME **SOUND EFFECTS**, ESPECIALLY IF IT'S A FIGHT SCENE!

ZAP ZATT!

STORY STARTERS

WRITING A COMIC CAN BE HARD. SO HERE'S A FEW STORY PROMPTS TO HELP YOU ON YOUR WAY.

A NOBLE QUEST

LET'S DESTROY THE NECROMANCER'S LAIR BEFORE EVIL CONSUMES THE WORLD!

A MISSION OF VENGEANCE

THAT NECROMANCER OWES ME TEN QUID. **GET HIM!!!**

A BATTLE AGAINST INVADERS

AAIIIIIEEE! HIDEOUS ALIENS FROM VENUS ARE ATTACKING!

WE'RE FROM MILTON KEYNES ACTUALLY, YOU ROTTER!

A HUNT FOR TREASURE

HA! THERE'S ONLY A BIG LIZARD GUARDING THE GOLD. THIS'LL BE A CINCH.

A HUNT FOR A MISSING PERSON

...

ALRIGHT, WHO STOLE THE OTHER PUPPET?

A FIGHT AGAINST IMPOSSIBLE ODDS

IT'S TIME FOR THE ELDER GODS TO RISE, AND SHOW THE WORLD THE WAY OF THE **KUNG FU!**

YOU'LL HAVE TO DEFEAT **ME** FIRST!

YEAH! SHE'S GOT A **STICK!**

A RACE FOR SURVIVAL

EEP!

DID I MENTION THAT IF YOU LOSE THE RACE, I GAIN POSSESSION OF YOUR MORTAL SOUL?

BRRRMMM!

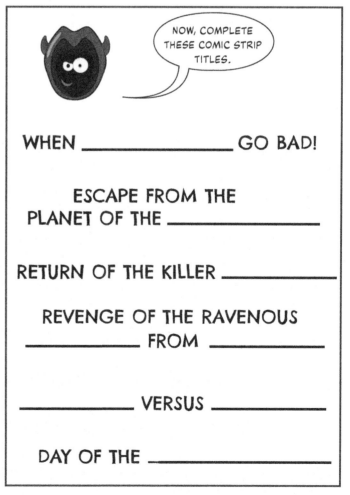

NOW, COMPLETE THESE COMIC STRIP TITLES.

WHEN _____ GO BAD!

ESCAPE FROM THE PLANET OF THE _____

RETURN OF THE KILLER _____

REVENGE OF THE RAVENOUS _____ FROM _____

_____ VERSUS _____

DAY OF THE _____

ONE LAST THING BEFORE YOU GET STARTED... NO COMIC IS COMPLETE WITHOUT AN EYE CATCHING COVER.

THE COVER IS SPLIT INTO **THREE** SECTIONS.

GALACTIC COMIX

ATTACK OF THE 7 EYED SPACE WOBBLER!

1 LOGO.

2 TITLE.

3 MAIN IMAGE.

TEST A FEW OF YOUR COVER DESIGN IDEAS BELOW, BEFORE YOU DRAW THE FINAL ONE ON THE NEXT PAGE.

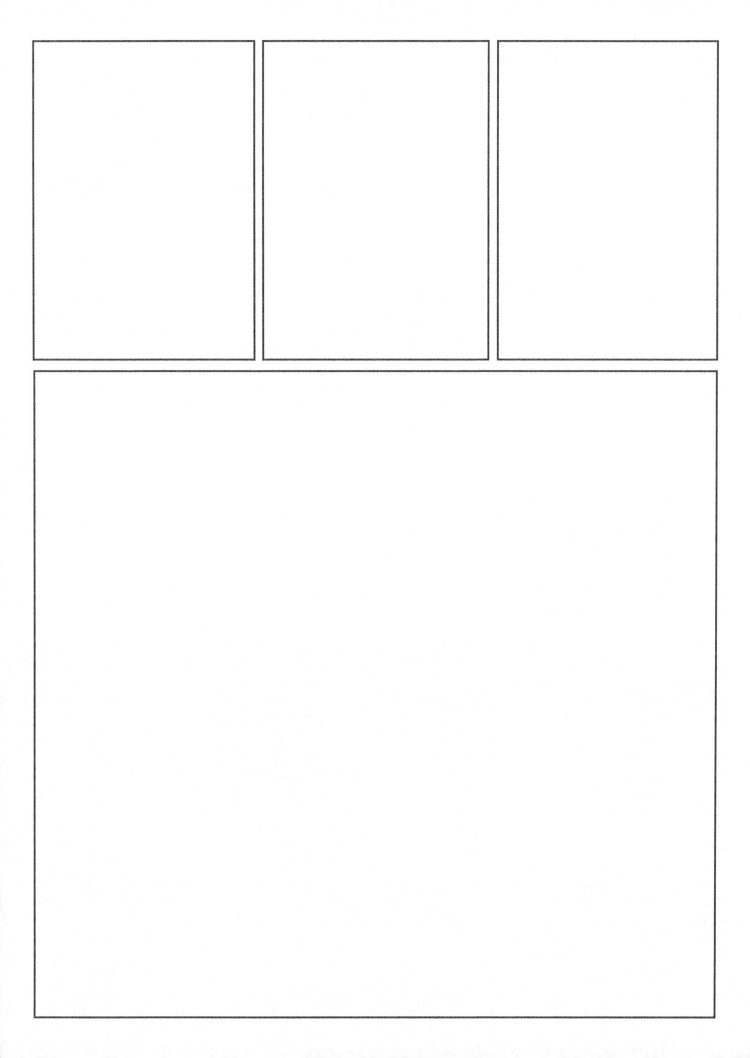

WELCOME! IN THIS SECTION YOU'LL FIND HALF A DOZEN BOARD HORDE 'ROLL AND DRAW' ADVENTURE GAMES, PLUS THE SUPPORTING MATERIAL FOR THE BOARD HORDE BOARD GAME (SOME OF WHICH CAN BE FOUND ON THE BACK COVER).

YOU CAN ALSO DOWNLOAD A PRINT AND PLAY VERSION OF THE MAIN BOARD GAME AT **WWW.DAVIDHAILWOOD.COM** ALONG WITH PLENTY OF EXTRA MATERIAL.

TO PLAY THE ROLL AND DRAW QUESTS YOU'LL NEED A PENCIL, AN ERASER, AND A DICE.

THE QUESTS ARE BEST PLAYED IN ORDER AS SOME REWARD YOU WITH GOLD, WHICH CAN BE USED TO MAKE PURCHASES THAT HELP YOU COMPLETE LATER QUESTS.

HIRE ME! I'M CRAZY CHEAP!

THE ADVENTURES ALL TAKE PLACE ON A 6 X 6 BOARD GRID WHICH IS NAVIGATED BY ROLLING A DICE.

RULES ON THE LEFT SIDE

BOARD ON THE RIGHT

YOU'LL MOSTLY BE PROMPTED TO DRAW HEROES AND SOMETIMES EVEN MONSTERS ON THE BOARD. THE DRAWINGS CAN BE AS DETAILED OR AS BASIC AS YOU LIKE -- YOU CAN EVEN USE STICK FIGURES!

GOOD LUCK ON YOUR QUESTS! AND DON'T WORRY IF YOU DON'T WIN EVERY TIME - YOU CAN ALWAYS USE AN ERASER AND TRY AGAIN.

HOW TO PLAY

1 Roll A Dice

This is the first number of the board square

eg:

3 and 1 means you look for square 3.1 (all squares are numbered in their top left corner)

2 Roll the Dice again

This is the second number of the board square

eg:

3 If the square is blank, either:

a) Draw a hero in it, from those available in the Hero Section beneath the board.

or b) Change the dice result using a Hero's power.

Hero powers are located in the Hero Section. The Mage and Rogue's powers can help you avoid landing on bad squares (Trap!) or find better squares (Treasure!)

ROGUE	MAGE
May change the order of dice rolls when moving	May reroll one of the dice when moving
REORDERS LEFT:	**MOVEMENT REROLLS:**

If you use a Hero's power you must put an X in their power bar, and draw a Hero in the new square (if it's blank). Hero powers can be used as many times in a row as you like, until they run out.

The Rogue has the power to reorder the dice. Eg:

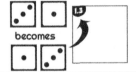

becomes

The Mage has the power to reroll one of the movement dice. Eg:

Rerolls the 1st dice   Rerolls the 2nd dice

might become   might become

4 If the square contains Treasure:

a) Put an X in the box beneath the square's number to show the Treasure has been claimed.

b) Roll a dice.

c) Note down the number of coins gained here.

5 If the square contains a Trap, either use a Hero's power to avoid landing on that square, or try to disarm it:

a) Roll a dice

b) If your roll is equal to or higher than the Trap's Strength (3 in this example), the Trap is disarmed, and you put an X in the box beneath the square's number.

c) If the number you roll is lower than the Trap's Strength you lose a life. Put an X through a heart in the Heroes lives bar.

LIVES

---

6 If the square contains a Beast, either use a Hero's power to avoid landing on that square, or attack it:

a) Roll a dice

b) The Beast's strength is shown on the dice at bottom of the Beast square. If your roll is equal to or higher than the Beast's strength (4 in this example), the Beast is defeated, and you put an X in the box beneath the square's number.

WARRIOR	May reroll the dice during combat
COMBAT REROLLS:	

c) If the number you roll is lower than the Beast's strength, either use the Warrior Hero's power to reroll the dice, or lose a life (put an X through either the Warrior's power, or through a heart in the Heroes lives bar).

7 If the square contains a Hero you've drawn, Treasure you've collected, Disarmed Trap or Defeated Beast, either use a Hero's power to avoid that square, or let your Heroes rest:

Either a) Recover a life (unless full). Erase an X from a heart in the Lives bar.

or b) Recover a power (unless full). Erase an X from one of the Hero's power bars.

8 Repeat from Step 1 until Victory or Defeat (see below)

VICTORY CONDITIONS

To Win Have an unbroken line of heroes leading from Entrance 1.1 to Exit 6.6 (the line doesn't need to be straight, but cannot be diagonal). Squares containing crossed through boxes (such as disarmed traps and defeated beasts) count as part of the line.

ENTRANCE ➡

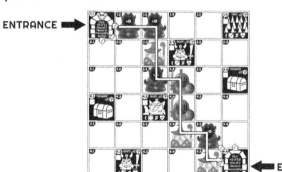

⬅ EXIT

On completion of the quest, add any treasure gained to the gold pouch at the bottom of this board and the next quest's board (Gold carries over from one quest to the next).

GOLD

Defeat If you run out of lives, it's game over!

HERO SECTION

ROGUE	MAGE	WARRIOR	LIVES	
May change the order of dice rolls when moving	May reroll one of the dice when moving	May reroll the dice during combat		GOLD
REORDERS LEFT:	MOVEMENT REROLLS:	COMBAT REROLLS:		

ROLL	DRAW	USE	COLLECT	AVOID/DEFEAT	ESCAPE
QUICK GUIDE					

HOW TO PLAY

Overview: Your Heroes now have a sleeping Dragon to contend with! Fortunately, a Bard is available from the Hero For Hire section beneath the board to reduce the chances of the Dragon awakening. **To Hire A Bard:** Pay 2 coins from your gold pouch (if you have enough) and put an X in the Hired box. Whenever you roll the number of a Board Square with Musical Notes in the corner, you may draw a Bard (other Heroes drawn here have no effect on the Dragon).

① Roll A Dice
This is the first number of the board square
eg: [⚁]

② Roll the Dice again
This is the second number of the board square
eg: [⚀]

3 and 1 means you look for square 3.1

③ If the square is blank or contains musical notes, either:
a) Draw a hero in it, from those available.

or b) **Change the dice result using a Hero's power.**
Hero powers are located in the Hero Section. The Mage and Rogue's powers can help you avoid landing on bad squares (Dragon!) or find better squares (Treasure!)

ROGUE	MAGE
May change the order of dice rolls when moving	May reroll one of the dice when moving
REORDERS LEFT:	**MOVEMENT REROLLS:**
✸ ✸ ✸	✸ ✸ ✸

If you use a Hero's power you must put an X in their power bar, and draw a Hero in the new square (if it's blank). Hero powers can be used as many times in a row as you like, until they run out.

④ If the square contains Treasure:
a) Put an X in the box beneath the square's number to show the Treasure has been claimed.
b) Roll a dice.
c) Note down the number of coins gained here.

⑤ If the square contains a Trap, either use a Hero's power to avoid landing on that square, or try to disarm it:
a) Roll a dice
b) If your roll is equal to or higher than the Trap's Strength (3 in this example), the Trap is disarmed, and you put an X in the box beneath the square's number.
c) If the number you roll is lower than the Trap's Strength you lose a life. Put an X through a heart in the Heroes lives bar.

⑥ If the square contains a Dragon, either use a Hero's power to avoid landing on that square, or:
a) Roll a dice twice, and add the numbers.
Eg: [⚀] + [⚄] = 6
b) Add 1 for every treasure collected. Eg:

6+3=9
c) Deduct 1 for every Musical Note square in which you've drawn a Bard hero (available from the Hero For Hire section).

d) If the final number adds up to 13 or more, the Dragon awakens and you lose! Otherwise you're safe for now.

3.3/3.4/4.3/4.4 DRAGON!
If you land here, roll 2 dice (or 1 dice twice). Add 1 for every collected treasure. Deduct any -1 squares with Bards in them (their soothing music helps keep the beast asleep). On a roll of 13+ the Dragon awakens!

⑦ If the square contains a Hero you've drawn, Treasure you've collected, or Disarmed Trap, either use a Hero's power to avoid that square, or let your Heroes rest:
Either a) Recover a life (unless full). Erase an X from a heart in the Lives bar. ♥
or b) Recover a power (unless full). Erase an X from one of the Hero's power bars. ✸

⑧ Repeat from Step 1 until Victory or Defeat (see below)

VICTORY CONDITIONS

To Win Collect all 8 Treasures, or have an unbroken line of heroes leading from Entrance 1.1 to Exit 6.6 (the line doesn't need to be straight, but cannot be diagonal). Squares containing crossed through boxes (such as disarmed Traps and plundered Treasure) count as part of the line.

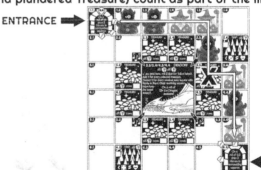

Add any Treasure gained to the gold pouch at the bottom of this board and the next quest's board. ➡

Defeat Wake the Dragon or run out of lives, game over!

1.1 On a roll of 1.1 draw 3 Heroes in surrounding squares

1.2

1.3

1.4

1.5

1.6

2.1

2.2

2.3 TREASURE! COINS:

2.4 TREASURE! COINS:

2.5

2.6 TRAP!

3.1

3.2 TREASURE! COINS:

3.3/3.4/4.3/4.4 DRAGON!
If you land here, roll 2 dice (or 1 dice twice). Add 1 for every collected treasure. Deduct 1 for every musical note square with Bards in them (their soothing music helps keep the beast asleep). On a roll of 13+ the Dragon awakens!

3.5 TREASURE! COINS: 1

3.6

4.1

4.2 TREASURE! COINS: 2

4.5 TREASURE! COINS:

4.6

5.1

5.2

5.3 TREASURE! COINS:

5.4 TREASURE! COINS:

5.5

5.6

6.1

6.2 TRAP!

6.3

6.4

6.5

6.6 On a roll of 6.6 draw 3 Heroes in surrounding squares

HERO SECTION

ROGUE — May change the order of dice rolls when moving
REORDERS LEFT:

MAGE — May reroll one of the dice when moving
MOVEMENT REROLLS:

LIVES

GOLD

HERO FOR HIRE

BARD — Soothes the Dragon when drawn on musical note squares
G2 HIRED

QUICK GUIDE

 ROLL
 DRAW
 USE
 COLLECT
 AVOID/DISARM
 AVOID ESCAPE

HOW TO PLAY

Overview: There are 7 Beasts for your Heroes to defeat. Some squares contain 2 Beasts, which need to be defeated one after the other (you can tell these apart from the single Beast squares, as they have 2 tick boxes).

There's a new easier way to defeat Beasts (as well as the old way). If you surround a Beast square by drawing your Heroes in all 3 adjacent squares (as shown in the squares top right corner) then all Beasts in the surrounded square are immediately defeated without the need to land on their square and roll a combat dice.

 Draw a Rogue when you land on a square with the Rogue symbol in the corner

 Draw a Warrior when you land on a square with the Warrior symbol in the corner

Draw a Mage when you land on a square with the Mage symbol in the corner

Once you've drawn all 3 Heroes, the surrounded Beast (or Beasts) is instantly defeated

① Roll A Dice
This is the first number of the board square

eg:

② Roll the Dice again
This is the second number of the board square

eg:

3 and 1 means you look for square 3.1

③ If the square is blank, either:
a) Draw a hero in it, from those available in the Hero Section.

or b) Change the dice result using a Hero's power.

Hero powers are located in the Hero Section. The Mage and Rogue's powers can help you avoid landing on bad squares (Trap!) or find better squares (Treasure!)

ROGUE	
	May change the order of dice rolls when moving
REORDERS LEFT:	

MAGE	
	May reroll one of the dice when moving
MOVEMENT REROLLS:	

If you use a Hero's power you must put an X in their power bar, and draw a Hero in the new square (if it's blank). Hero powers can be used as many times in a row as you like, until they run out.

④ If the square contains Treasure:
a) Put an X in the box beneath the square's number to show the Treasure has been claimed.

b) Roll a dice.

c) Note down the number of coins gained here.

⑤ If the square contains a Trap, either use a Hero's power to avoid landing on that square, or try to disarm it:
a) Roll a dice

b) If your roll is equal to or higher than the Trap's Strength (3 in this example), the Trap is disarmed, and you put an X in the box beneath the square's number.

c) If the number you roll is lower than the Trap's Strength you lose a life. Put an X through a heart in the Heroes lives bar.

⑥ If the square contains a Beast, either use a Hero's power to avoid landing on that square, or attack it:
a) Roll a dice

b) The Beast's strength is shown on the dice at bottom of the Beast square. If your roll is equal to or higher than the Beast's strength (4 in this example), the Beast is defeated, and you put an X in the box beneath the square's number.

WARRIOR	
	May reroll the dice during combat
COMBAT REROLLS:	

c) If the number you roll is lower than the Beast's strength, either use the Warrior Hero's power to reroll the dice, or lose a life (put an X through either the Warrior's power, or through a heart in the Heroes lives bar).

Don't forget: If a Beast displays 2 tick boxes, then there's 2 Beasts in that square to be defeated (the second Beast cannot be attacked until you've defeated the first).

⑦ If the square contains a Hero you've drawn, Treasure you've collected, Disarmed Trap or Defeated Beast, either use a Hero's power to avoid that square, or let your Heroes rest:

Either a) Recover a life (unless full). Erase an X from a heart in the Lives bar.

or b) Recover a power (unless full). Erase an X from one of the Hero's power bars.

⑧ Repeat from Step 1 until Victory or Defeat (see below)

VICTORY CONDITIONS

To Win Surround or defeat all 7 Monsters.

Add any treasure gained to the gold pouch at the bottom of this board and the next quest's board. ➡

Defeat If you lose all 3 lives, it's game over!

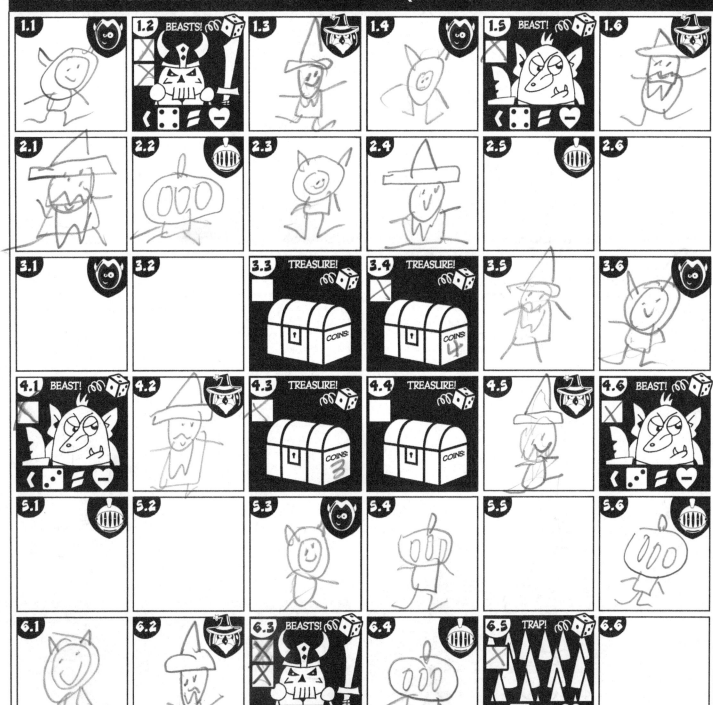

HERO SECTION

ROGUE	MAGE	WARRIOR	LIVES
May change the order of dice rolls when moving	May reroll one of the dice when moving	May reroll the dice during combat	
REORDERS LEFT:	**MOVEMENT REROLLS:**	**COMBAT REROLLS:**	**GOLD**

ROLL   DRAW   USE   COLLECT   AVOID/DISARM   SURROUND/DEFEAT

QUICK GUIDE

HOW TO PLAY

Overview: Lead the Miners to safety, grab the loot, or do a bit of both. Every Rock and Treasure you collect increases the chances of a Cave In. Fortunately, an Alchemist is available from the Hero For Hire section beneath the board to help increase your survival odds.

 To Hire An Alchemist: Pay 10 coins from your gold pouch (if you have enough) and put an X in the Hired box. Whenever you fail a Cave In check, the Alchemist allows you to reroll the dice (to a maximum of 3 times).

1 Roll A Dice

This is the first number of the board square
eg:

2 Roll the Dice again
This is the second number of the board square
eg:

3 and 1 means you look for square 3.1 (all squares are numbered in their top left corner)

3 If the square is blank, either:
a) Draw a hero in it, from those available in the Hero Section beneath the board.

or b) Change the dice result using a Hero's power.

Hero powers are located in the Hero Section. The Mage and Rogue's powers can help you avoid landing on bad squares, or find better squares.

ROGUE		MAGE	
	May change the order of dice rolls when moving		May reroll one of the dice when moving
REORDERS LEFT:		**MOVEMENT REROLLS:**	

If you use a Hero's power you must put an X in their power bar, and draw a Hero in the new square (if it's blank). Hero powers can be used as many times in a row as you like, until they run out.

The Rogue has the power to reorder the dice. Eg:
becomes

The Mage has the power to reroll one of the movement dice. Eg:
Rerolls the 1st dice   Rerolls the 2nd dice
might become   might become

4 If the square contains Treasure, either use a Hero's power to avoid landing on that square, or:

a) Put an X in the box beneath the square's number to show the Treasure has been claimed.

b) Roll a dice and note down the number of coins gained.

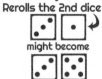

5 If the square contains a Rock Pile, either use a Hero's power to avoid landing on that square, or:
a) Put an X in the box beneath the square's number to show the Rock Pile has been removed.
b) Perform a **Cave In check**: Roll 2 dice and add 1 for every Rock Pile removed and Treasure collected (If you've hired an Alchemist, you may reroll the dice).

Eg:

c) If the final number adds up to 14 or more, a Cave In happens!

6 If the square contains a Miner:
Each time you land on a Miner you may remove 1 adjacent Rock Pile (to his left, right, above or below), without having to perform a Cave In check (put an X in its box).

Can remove one or the other.

7 If the square already contains a Hero you've drawn, or Treasure/Rock Pile you've collected, either use a Hero's power to avoid that square, or let your Heroes rest: Erase an X from one of the Hero's power bars (unless full).

8 Repeat from Step 1 until Victory or Defeat (see below)

VICTORY CONDITIONS

To Win Either: have an unbroken line of heroes leading from each Miner to the Exit (the line doesn't need to be straight, but cannot be diagonal. The Miner's lines do not need to connect to each other). Squares containing crossed through boxes (such as removed rocks and collected Treasures) count as part of the line.

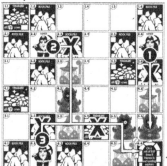

◄— EXIT

Or: Collect all 4 Treasures.
On completion of the quest, add any Treasure gained to the gold pouch at the bottom of this board and ➡ the next quest's board.

Defeat If you cause a Cave In, it's game over!

BOARD HORDE ROLL AND DRAW   QUEST 4: RESCUE THE MINERS (AND THEIR GOLD)

1.1 TREASURE! COINS:	**1.2** ROCK PILE — CAVE IN CHECK!	**1.3**	**1.4**	**1.5**	**1.6** ROCK PILE — CAVE IN CHECK!
2.1 ROCK PILE — CAVE IN CHECK!	**2.2** MINER	**2.3** ROCK PILE — CAVE IN CHECK!	**2.4**	**2.5** ROCK PILE — CAVE IN CHECK!	**2.6** MINER
3.1	**3.2** ROCK PILE — CAVE IN CHECK!	**3.3**	**3.4**	**3.5** TREASURE! COINS: 6	**3.6** ROCK PILE — CAVE IN CHECK!
4.1 TREASURE! COINS:	**4.2**	**4.3**	**4.4**	**4.5**	**4.6**
5.1	**5.2** ROCK PILE — CAVE IN CHECK!	**5.3**	**5.4** TREASURE! COINS: 6	**5.5**	**5.6**
6.1 ROCK PILE — CAVE IN CHECK!	**6.2** MINER	**6.3** ROCK PILE — CAVE IN CHECK!	**6.4**	**6.5**	**6.6** On a roll of 6.6 draw 3 Heroes in surrounding squares

HERO SECTION   HERO FOR HIRE

ROGUE — May change the order of dice rolls when moving
REORDERS LEFT:

MAGE — May reroll one of the dice when moving
MOVEMENT REROLLS:

GOLD

ALCHEMIST — G10 — HIRED — May reroll the dice when performing a Cave In check
USES LEFT:

QUICK GUIDE

ROLL	DRAW	USE	COLLECT	REMOVE	RESCUE	AVOID

HOW TO PLAY

Overview: This Quest works a bit differently to the others, as you're using powerful spells to attack Beasts. Whenever you miss, another Beast spawns! Fortunately there are spare power charges available to buy from a shop, should you ever run out.

1 Roll A Dice
This is the first number of the board square
eg: [die showing 3]

2 Roll the Dice again
This is the second number of the board square
eg: [die showing 1]

3 If the square contains a Beast:
(including ones you've drawn)

Direct hit! Put an X in its box, and recover a power charge (unless full).

4 If the square is empty:
Your Mage's opening attack has missed!
Either a) draw a Beast in the blank square.
Or b) Use one of the Mage's special powers to hit a Beast in a square adjacent to the one you rolled, and lose a power charge.

MAGE		SPECIAL POWERS	
[Mage image]	**POWER CHARGES** [row of power charges]	**3 SQUARE HORIZONTAL BLAST** X X X — Hits the square rolled, and the squares to its left and right	**3 SQUARE VERTICAL BLAST** X / X / X — Hits the square rolled, and the squares above and below it.

Mage's special powers are located in the Hero Section, beneath the board squares.

Vertical Blast Example: If you rolled 4 and 6 on the dice, square 4.6 is empty and it's a miss. However, you could use a Vertical Blast to hit any Beasts in the squares above and below 4.6. As the square below 4.6 contains a Beast, you would put an X in its box (it has been defeated) and put an X through a Mage power charge. Now you've hit a Beast, there's no need to draw a new one in the empty square (this helps keep the Beasts from spreading).

Horizontal Blast Example

This works in the same way as a Vertical Blast, except horizontally. Here, if you rolled a 2 and a 2 you could use a Vertical Blast to hit the squares to its left and right, destroying the Beast in 2.1.

5 If the square contains the Mage's Tower (it takes up 4 squares), or a Defeated Beast:
Your Mage rests and recovers a power charge (unless full). Erase an X from a power charge in the Mage's power bar.

6 If you run out of Power Charges:
SHOP   **G 3 EACH**   If you have enough gold, you can buy more Power Charges at the Tower's Shop (located in the Hero Section) for 3 Gold each. Put an X in the shop tick box, and erase an X from your Mage's Power Charges for each purchase (you can buy as many as you want) and deduct the cost from your gold pouch.

7 Repeat from Step 1 until Victory or Defeat (see below)

VICTORY CONDITIONS

To Win Defeat 10 Beasts (or every Beast on the board, if there's less than 10).
On completion of the quest, transfer your remaining gold to the gold pouch on the next quest's board. →

Defeat If the tower gets surrounded (Beasts in all 12 squares around it. Even defeated beasts count) it's game over!

Also, if at any point there are 12 or more *living* beasts anywhere on the board, the Mage's tower gets overrun and it's game over!

1.1

1.2

1.3

1.4

1.5

1.6

2.1 BEAST!

2.2

2.3

2.4 BEAST!

2.5

2.6

3.1

3.2

3.3/3.4/4.3/4.4 MAGE'S TOWER

If you land here, rest and recover a power charge (unless they're full).

3.5

3.6

4.1

4.2 BEAST!

4.5

4.6

5.1

5.2

5.3

5.4

5.5

5.6 BEAST!

6.1

6.2 BEAST!

6.3

6.4

6.5

6.6

HERO SECTION   SPECIAL POWERS   SHOP 🪙 3 EACH

MAGE
POWER CHARGES

3 SQUARE HORIZONTAL BLAST
X X X
Hits the square rolled, and the squares to its left and right.

3 SQUARE VERTICAL BLAST
X
X
X
Hits the square rolled, and the squares above and below it.

GOLD

Extra Power Charges

ROLL   DEFEAT   USE   MISS? DRAW

QUICK GUIDE

BOARD HORDE ROLL AND DRAW

QUEST 6: HOLD BACK THE HORDE

HOW TO PLAY

Overview: Your final task is to stop the Horde from reaching the city at the top of the board, by placing Heroes, attacking Beasts and building/fortifying Defences.

To the left of the board, there are 6 hourglasses (one for each row). The bottoms of the hourglasses are split into 6 numbered segments, which track the number of turns until the Horde advances into that row.

Below the board is a Horde of Beasts, some of which are stronger than others. At the start of the game, they're not on the board, but you'll be drawing their advance as the game progresses.

1 At the start of your first turn, or if the Horde has advanced a row (otherwise skip this step):

Roll a Dice and write the number in the top of the hourglass which stands above the Horde row (eg, if its your first go, you would use the hourglass next to row 6. If the Horde advanced into row 6 at the end of the previous turn, you would use the hourglass next to row 5).

When the Time Tracker reaches the same number as the top of the hourglass, the Horde advances into the next row (you'll be shading the segments in during the Time Advances step).

2 Roll A Dice	**3** Roll the Dice again	**4** If the square is blank or contains an Extra Time symbol:
This is the first number of the board square.	This is the second number of the board square.	Either a) Draw a hero in it. b) Draw defences in it.
eg: 	eg:	

3 and 1 means you look for square 3.1

or c) Change the dice result using a Hero's power.

Hero powers are located in the Hero Section. The Mage and Rogue's powers can help you avoid landing on bad squares, or find better squares.

If you use a Hero's power you must put an X in their power bar, and draw a Hero or Defence in the new square (if it's blank). Hero powers can be used as many times in a row as you like, until they run out.

If at any point you manage to draw a Hero behind a Defence, or a Defence in front of a Hero, that board column is considered **Fortified** and the Horde can no longer advance into that column's squares (put an X in the 'Fortified' tick box in the City square at the top of the column).

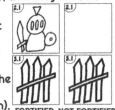

5 If the square already contains Defences or a Hero:

You may draw a Hero in the square behind the defences, or draw defences in the square in front of the Hero, if it's empty. This column is now **Fortified** against the Horde, and they're unable to advance into it (put an X in the 'Fortified' tick box in the City square at the top of the column).

If you're unable to do either, you may instead choose to recover a life, or recover a power (unless they're full). ♥ ✸

6 If the square contains a Beast, either use a Hero's power to avoid landing on that square, or attack it:

a) Roll a dice

b) The Beast's strength is shown on the dice of the Horde at the bottom of the column. If your roll is equal to or higher than the Beast's strength (3 in this example), the Beast is defeated. Erase the Beast and draw a Hero or Defences in its place.

c) If the number you roll is lower than the Beast's strength, either use the Warrior Hero's power to reroll the dice, or lose a life (put an X through either the Warrior's power, or through a heart in the Heroes lives bar).

7 If the square contains a City, either use a Hero's power to avoid landing on that square or let your Heroes rest:

Either a) Recover a life (unless full). Erase an X from a heart in the Heroes lives bar.

b) Recover a power (unless full). Erase an X from a Hero's power bar.

8 **Extra Time** If you drew a Hero or Defences in a square with an Extra Time symbol, there is no need to advance the Time Tracker at the end of this turn.

You can also try to gain Extra Time at the end of each turn by Playing The Reaper: Roll a dice

1-3 you lose a life

4+ = Extra Time. No need to advance the Time Tracker.

9 **Time Advances**

At the end of your turn (after you've drawn a Hero, attacked a Beast, etc) unless you've been rewarded with Extra Time, shade in the next segment of the active hourglass. If the number of the segment shaded matches the number in the top of the hourglass, the Horde advances (see below). Otherwise, repeat from Step 2

10 **The Horde Advances**

To advance the Horde, draw a Beast in all free spaces of the row in which the hourglass ran out (except in columns which have been Fortified). Put an X through the top of the hourglass.

If there is a Hero or Defence in the square (and the Column is Unfortified):

For now, the Horde cannot advance into that square. However, when the Horde next advances, they will fill any empty space behind the Hero/Defence (unless you fill it first!).

If there is a City in the square that the Horde has advanced into: The Horde has won!

11 Repeat from Step 1 until Victory or Defeat (see below)

VICTORY CONDITIONS

To Win Stop the Horde's advance before it reaches the city by building a defence with a Hero behind it in all 6 columns.

Defeat If the Horde advances into the city when the last Time Tracker runs out, or if you run out of lives, it's game over!

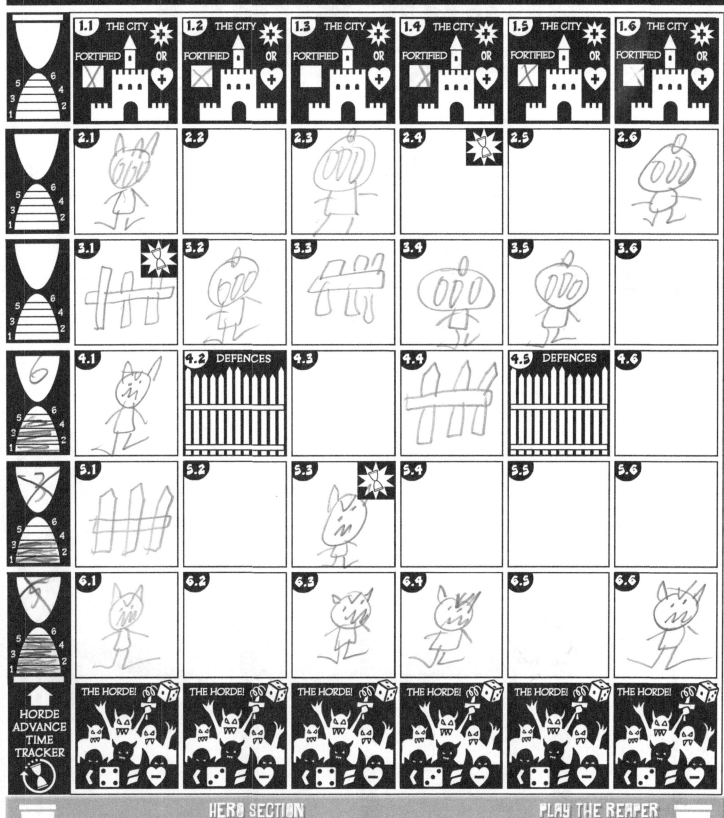

1.1 THE CITY — FORTIFIED **OR**
1.2 THE CITY — FORTIFIED **OR**
1.3 THE CITY — FORTIFIED **OR**
1.4 THE CITY — FORTIFIED **OR**
1.5 THE CITY — FORTIFIED **OR**
1.6 THE CITY — FORTIFIED **OR**

2.1 · **2.2** · **2.3** · **2.4** · **2.5** · **2.6**

3.1 · **3.2** · **3.3** · **3.4** · **3.5** · **3.6**

4.1 · **4.2** DEFENCES · **4.3** · **4.4** · **4.5** DEFENCES · **4.6**

5.1 · **5.2** · **5.3** · **5.4** · **5.5** · **5.6**

6.1 · **6.2** · **6.3** · **6.4** · **6.5** · **6.6**

HORDE ADVANCE TIME TRACKER

THE HORDE! · THE HORDE! · THE HORDE! · THE HORDE! · THE HORDE! · THE HORDE!

HERO SECTION

ROGUE — May change the order of dice rolls when moving
REORDERS LEFT:

MAGE — May reroll one of the dice when moving
MOVEMENT REROLLS:

WARRIOR — May reroll the dice during combat
COMBAT REROLLS:

LIVES

GOLD

PLAY THE REAPER

WIN EXTRA TIME

Board Horde can be played by 2 or 3 players, using the materials provided (Heroes, Tokens and Monsters can be found on the back cover. Hero Sheets, Boards and Scoreboard can be found after these Rules). You will also need a 6 sided dice (not included)

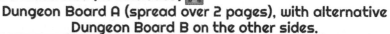

Dungeon Board A (spread over 2 pages), with alternative Dungeon Board B on the other sides.

3 Blue Team Heroes

| ROGUE | WARRIOR | MAGE |

3 Red Team Heroes

| ROGUE | WARRIOR | MAGE |

3 Purple Team Heroes

| ROGUE | WARRIOR | MAGE |

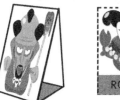

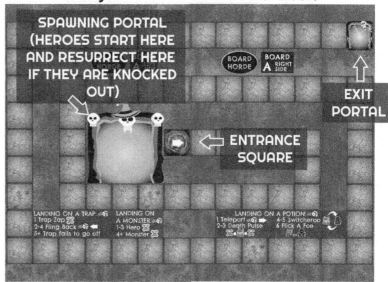

SPAWNING PORTAL (HEROES START HERE AND RESURRECT HERE IF THEY ARE KNOCKED OUT)

BOARD HORDE — BOARD A RIGHT SIDE

EXIT PORTAL

⬅ ENTRANCE SQUARE

LANDING ON A TRAP
1 Trap Zap
2-4 Fling Back
5+ Trap fails to go off

LANDING ON A MONSTER
1-3 Hero
4+ Monster

LANDING ON A POTION
1 Teleport   4-5 Switcheroo
2-3 Death Pulse   6 Flick A Foe

4 x Monsters

| MONSTER | MONSTER | MONSTER | MONSTER |

4 Potion Tokens   **4 Trap Tokens**   **3 Special Items**

3 x Double Sided Hero Sheets (1 Blue Team, 1 Red Team, 1 Purple Team) with Standard and Advanced sides.

12 x Claimed Trap Markers (4 Blue, 4 Red, 4 Purple)

12 Tamed Monster Markers (4 Blue, 4 Red, 4 Purple)

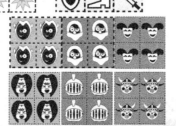

3 x Grim Score keepers

| GRIM SCORE KEEPER | GRIM SCORE KEEPER | GRIM SCORE KEEPER |

Scoreboard

BOARD HORDE RULES   SETUP

- ◆ Place the board on a flat surface (table or floor) on the Board A side (Board B setup changes are covered on the last page of the rules).

- ◆ Place the Heroes (3 for each player) in the Spawning Portal.

- ◆ Place the Grim Score Keepers on the Scoreboard's '0' square.

- ◆ Place 4 Monsters, Potion Tokens and Trap Tokens on random board squares (anywhere but the Entrance Square, Exit Portal, or first 6 Squares) making sure to space them out a bit.

- ◆ Either A) Place the 3 Special Item Tokens on random empty board squares (anywhere but the Entrance Square, Exit Portal, or first 6 squares) making sure to space them out a bit.

- ◆ Or B) Place the 3 Special Item Tokens in a stack on an empty square in the middle of the board.

- ◆ Place the Hero Sheets for Blue Team, Red Team and Purple Team (if they're playing) next to each player, making sure they're on the same side (Standard or Advanced).

- ◆ Place the Claimed Trap Markers and Tamed Monster Markers in their assigned places on the Rogue and Warrior sections of the Hero Sheets.

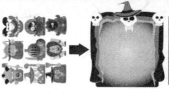
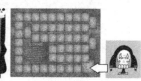

ROGUE MARKERS Place Rogue Marker below, for use when CLAIMING a Trap. ➡ **WARRIOR MARKERS** Place Warrior Marker below, for use when TAMING a Monster. ➡

Now you have finished setting up, players roll a dice to see who goes first (highest number rolled wins).

GOAL OF THE GAME

Board Horde is a competetive dice rolling dungeon crawler. The goal is to get your 3 Heroes (a Rogue, a Warrior and a Mage) to the Exit before your opponent(s), avoiding Traps and Monsters.

ROLL   MOVE   DRINK   COLLECT   AVOID OR   AVOID OR   ESCAPE

DISARM   ATTACK

ORDER OF PLAY

Unless choosing to use a stored Potion (see Potions section) the player whose turn it is rolls a 6 sided dice.

FIRST GO (OR IF THERE ARE NO HEROES FROM *ANY* SIDE LEFT ON THE BOARD)

Select one of your Heroes from the Spawning Portal and move them onto the board by the number of spaces shown on the dice.

ANY OTHER GO

ENTRANCE   SPAWNING
SQUARE   PORTAL

♦ On a roll of 1-5, select one of your Heroes who's already on the board and move them by the number of spaces shown on the dice.

♦ On a 6, you may choose to place a Hero from the Spawning Portal onto the Entrance Square, instead of moving (The more Heroes you have on the board at once, the better your chances of reaching the Exit). If an opponent's Hero is already on the Entrance Square, their Hero is knocked back into the Spawning Portal. If one of your own Heroes is already on the Entrance Square then you must move that Hero before bringing another out of the Spawning Portal.

♦ If you roll a 6 when all of your Heroes that haven't reached the exit are on the board (and not in the Spawning Portal), you get an extra movement dice roll.

MOVEMENT RULES

♦ A Hero cannot end its move on top of another of your own team's Heroes. If the path is blocked, you must move a different Hero.

♦ If your Hero ends its move on top of an opponent's Hero (and they're not carrying the Special Item 'Shield'), their Hero is knocked out and returns to the Spawning Portal.

SPACE FREE   BLOCKED

♦ If you land on a Trap, ⚡ Monster, 👹 Potion 🧪 or Special Item 🛡📜🗡 then refer to that section of the Rules to determine the result.

♦ If you land on or pass the Exit Portal, that Hero has escaped and is removed from the board.

♦ If all 3 of your Heroes reach the Exit Portal before your opponent(s), the game ends and the player with the highest score wins (see 'Scoring' below).

NONE OF YOUR OWN HEROES ARE LEFT ON THE BOARD

♦ If you have no Heroes left on the board, but some are still in the Spawning Portal (due to death by Monster, Trap, etc), on your turn you roll the dice 3 times. On a 6, you may place a Hero on the Entrance Square (the Hero cannot move until your next turn). If you fail to roll a 6, you must wait until your next turn to roll 3 times and try again.

♦ If by your third turn you have yet to roll a 6, you may place a Hero on the Entrance Square.

SCORING

♦ There's a scoreboard numbered 0 to 49 which is tended to by each team's Grim Score Keeper (if you make it past 49, the Reaper goes around the scoreboard again).

♦ Points are awarded for the following: Monster Defeated, Claimed or Tamed (3 pts) Trap Avoided, Claimed or Collected (2 pts) Potion Collected or Stored (1 pt) Special Item Collected (1 pt) Other Player's Hero Defeated (by landing on them, potion effect, etc) 3 pts. Exit Reached (10 pts)

♦ For a simpler game you can ignore the scoring, and play 'first person to get all 3 Heroes to the Exit wins'

CLASS: ROGUE / SKILL: DISARM TRAPS

SPECIAL ITEMS

Place below when a Rogue ends its turn on top of them. Dropped if that Hero is destroyed (by potion effect, Monster, Hero, or Trap).

 SWORD +1 to all combat dice rolls with this Hero

 SHOES Hero doesn't set off Traps (a Rogue may CLAIM or KEEP the trap).

 SHIELD A Hero with a shield is knocked back into the nearest free space when an opponent's Hero lands on them.

ROGUE MARKERS

Place Rogue Markers below, for use when CLAIMING a Trap.

TRAPS COLLECTED

+1 per Trap

If a Rogue avoids setting off a Trap, either CLAIM it, or KEEP it above.

If ANY of your Heroes (not just the Rogue) land on a Trap, add 1 to the dice roll for each Trap stacked here.

SUBCLASS: TRICKSTER — SPECIAL SKILL: SPEED BURST

The Trickster gives +1 to the movement dice roll for team mates stood in any square behind the Trickster (the +1 can be ignored if it leads to an unfavourable placement).

CLASS: MAGE / SKILL: COLLECT POTIONS

SPECIAL ITEMS

Place below when a Mage ends its turn on top of them. Dropped if that Hero is destroyed (by potion effect, Monster, Hero, or Trap).

 SWORD +1 to all combat dice rolls with this Hero

 SHOES This Hero doesn't set off any Traps

 SHIELD A Hero with a shield is knocked back into the nearest free space when an opponent's Hero lands on them.

POTIONS COLLECTED

Stack potions collected by the Mage here.

If a Mage lands on a Potion, either USE it straight away, or KEEP it for ANY of your Heroes on the board to use at the start of a later turn (remove potion after use).

ADVANCED PURPLE PLAYER HERO SHEET

SUBCLASS: NECROMANCER — SPECIAL SKILL: RESURRECT

Whenever any Hero on the Necromancer's side (including the Necromancer) makes a bad dice roll that would usually result in death, the Hero may reroll the dice (only once per turn, and the Necromancer MUST be on the board to use his skill).

Combat Roll

Opera Blast   Trap Roll

CLASS: WARRIOR / SKILL: TAME MONSTER

SPECIAL ITEMS

Place below when a Warrior ends its turn on top of them. Dropped if that Hero is destroyed (by potion effect, Monster, Hero, or Trap).

 SWORD +1 to all combat dice rolls with this Hero

 SHOES This Hero doesn't set off any Traps

 SHIELD A Hero with a shield is knocked back into the nearest free space when an opponent's Hero lands on them.

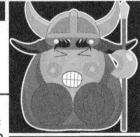

WARRIOR MARKERS

Place Warrior Markers below, for use when TAMING a Monster.

MONSTERS KEPT

+1 per Monster

+1 per Monster

+1 per Monster

+1 per Monster

SUBCLASS: VALKYRIE — SPECIAL SKILL: OPERA BLAST

Instead of moving, the Valkyrie can choose to release a deadly operatic blast. Roll a dice and remove any opposing team's Heroes within that range (counting from the Valkyrie's square forwards). On a 1 the Valkyrie destroys herself.

CLASS: ROGUE / SKILL: DISARM TRAPS

SPECIAL ITEMS

Place below when a Rogue ends its turn on top of them. Dropped if that Hero is destroyed (by potion effect, Monster, Hero, or Trap).

 SWORD +1 to all combat dice rolls with this Hero

 SHOES Hero doesn't set off Traps (a Rogue may CLAIM or KEEP the trap).

SHIELD A Hero with a shield is knocked back into the nearest free space when an opponent's Hero lands on them.

ROGUE MARKERS

Place Rogue Markers below, for use when CLAIMING a Trap.

TRAPS COLLECTED

+1 per Trap

If a Rogue avoids setting off a Trap, either CLAIM it, or KEEP it above.

If ANY of your Heroes (not just the Rogue) land on a Trap, add 1 to the dice roll for each Trap stacked here.

LANDING ON A TRAP

1 Trap Zap. Hero returns to the Spawning Portal to await resurrection.

2-4 Fling Back. Roll the dice again, and move your Hero backwards that amount of spaces (if you land on a Hero or Monster you're both destroyed).

5+ Trap fails to go off (you are safe). If your Hero is a Rogue, the trap is disarmed and you can either CLAIM or KEEP it.

Place a Rogue Marker on the Trap to CLAIM it. Your Heroes do not set off Traps that you've claimed when landed on.

Place the Trap in the Traps Collected area to the left to KEEP it. This gives ALL your Heroes a +1 dice roll bonus when they next land on a Trap (these bonuses stack).

If you claim or keep a trap already claimed by another player, their Rogue Marker is returned to them.

CLASS: MAGE / SKILL: COLLECT POTIONS

SPECIAL ITEMS

Place below when a Mage ends its turn on top of them. Dropped if that Hero is destroyed (by potion effect, Monster, Hero, or Trap).

 SWORD +1 to all combat dice rolls with this Hero

 SHOES This Hero doesn't set off any Traps

SHIELD A Hero with a shield is knocked back into the nearest free space when an opponent's Hero lands on them.

If a Mage lands on a Potion, either USE it straight away, or KEEP it for ANY of your Heroes on the board to use at the start of a later turn (remove potion after use).

STANDARD PURPLE PLAYER HERO SHEET

POTIONS COLLECTED

Stack potions collected by the Mage here.

LANDING ON A POTION

Potions are removed from the board after use. If a Mage lands on a potion, you can choose to COLLECT it for later use.

1 Teleport. Roll the dice again, and move your Hero forwards that number of spaces (if you land on a Hero, Monster or Potion it is destroyed).

2-3 Death Pulse. Any untamed Monster/other player's Hero in an adjacent square is destroyed and removed from the board (the other player's Hero is returned to the Spawning Portal)

4-5 Switcheroo. Switch places with another player's Hero, or Monster of your choice. If there aren't any Heroes or Monsters in front of you, the opportunity is lost and the potion removed.

6 Flick A Foe. Remove either another player's Hero or a Monster from the board (the Hero is returned to the Spawning Portal).

CLASS: WARRIOR / SKILL: TAME MONSTER

SPECIAL ITEMS

Place below when a Warrior ends its turn on top of them. Dropped if that Hero is destroyed (by potion effect, Monster, Hero, or Trap).

 SWORD +1 to all combat dice rolls with this Hero

 SHOES This Hero doesn't set off any Traps

SHIELD A Hero with a shield is knocked back into the nearest free space when an opponent's Hero lands on them.

WARRIOR MARKERS

Place Warrior Markers below, for use when TAMING a Monster.

MONSTERS KEPT

+1 per Monster

+1 per Monster

+1 per Monster

+1 per Monster

LANDING ON A MONSTER

1-3 The Monster defeats you. Place your Hero in the Spawning Portal to await resurrection.

4+ You defeat the Monster. Remove the Monster from the board, unless your Hero is a Warrior.

If your Hero is a Warrior, you can either TAME or KEEP the Monster.

Place a Warrior Marker on the Monster's board square to TAME it. You do not need to roll a dice if ANY of your Heroes land on this Monster.

Place the Monster in the Monsters Kept area to the left to KEEP it. This gives ALL your Heroes a +1 dice roll bonus when they next land on a Monster you haven't Tamed (these bonuses stack).

If you Tame, Keep or Defeat a Monster already Tamed by another player, their Warrior Marker is returned to them.

CLASS: ROGUE / SKILL: DISARM TRAPS

SPECIAL ITEMS

Place below when a Rogue ends its turn on top of them. Dropped if that Hero is destroyed (by potion effect, Monster, Hero, or Trap).

 SWORD +1 to all combat dice rolls with this Hero

 SHOES Hero doesn't set off Traps (a Rogue may CLAIM or KEEP the trap).

 SHIELD A Hero with a shield is knocked back into the nearest free space when an opponent's Hero lands on them.

ROGUE MARKERS

Place Rogue Markers below, for use when CLAIMING a Trap.

TRAPS COLLECTED

+1 per Trap

If a Rogue avoids setting off a Trap, either CLAIM it, or KEEP it above.

If ANY of your Heroes (not just the Rogue) land on a Trap, add 1 to the dice roll for each Trap stacked here.

SUBCLASS: ASSASSIN
SPECIAL SKILL: BACKSTAB

If the Assassin ends his turn on a square behind an untamed Monster or an opponent's Hero, he stabs them in the back (Monsters are removed from the board and Heroes are returned to the Spawning Portal)

CLASS: MAGE / SKILL: COLLECT POTIONS

SPECIAL ITEMS

Place below when a Mage ends its turn on top of them. Dropped if that Hero is destroyed (by potion effect, Monster, Hero, or Trap).

 SWORD +1 to all combat dice rolls with this Hero

 SHOES This Hero doesn't set off any Traps

 SHIELD A Hero with a shield is knocked back into the nearest free space when an opponent's Hero lands on them.

POTIONS COLLECTED

Stack potions collected by the Mage here.

If a Mage lands on a Potion, either USE it straight away, or KEEP it for ANY of your Heroes on the board to use at the start of a later turn (remove potion after use).

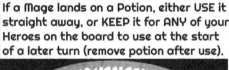

ADVANCED RED PLAYER HERO SHEET

SUBCLASS: WIZARD
SPECIAL SKILL: CURE

Whenever the Wizard is on the board (and not in the Spawning/Exit Portal), any Hero on his team that is slain (except himself) instantly resurrects on the Entrance Square, instead of returning to the Spawning Portal and having to roll a 6.

CLASS: WARRIOR / SKILL: TAME MONSTER

SPECIAL ITEMS

Place below when a Warrior ends its turn on top of them. Dropped if that Hero is destroyed (by potion effect, Monster, Hero, or Trap).

 SWORD +1 to all combat dice rolls with this Hero

 SHOES This Hero doesn't set off any Traps

 SHIELD A Hero with a shield is knocked back into the nearest free space when an opponent's Hero lands on them.

WARRIOR MARKERS

Place Warrior Markers below, for use when TAMING a Monster.

MONSTERS KEPT

+1 per Monster

+1 per Monster

+1 per Monster

+1 per Monster

SUBCLASS: KNIGHT
SPECIAL SKILL: SECOND WIND

If a Knight loses a Combat Roll when landing on a Monster, he gets to roll the dice a second time.

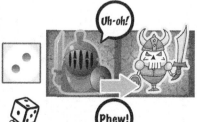

Uh-oh!

Phew!

CLASS: ROGUE / SKILL: DISARM TRAPS

SPECIAL ITEMS

Place below when a Rogue ends its turn on top of them. Dropped if that Hero is destroyed (by potion effect, Monster, Hero, or Trap).

 SWORD +1 to all combat dice rolls with this Hero

 SHOES Hero doesn't set off Traps (a Rogue may CLAIM or KEEP the trap).

 SHIELD A Hero with a shield is knocked back into the nearest free space when an opponent's Hero lands on them.

ROGUE MARKERS

Place Rogue Markers below, for use when CLAIMING a Trap.

TRAPS COLLECTED

+1 per Trap

If a Rogue avoids setting off a Trap, either CLAIM it, or KEEP it above.

If ANY of your Heroes (not just the Rogue) land on a Trap, add 1 to the dice roll for each Trap stacked here.

LANDING ON A TRAP

1 Trap Zap. Hero returns to the Spawning Portal to await resurrection.

2-4 Fling Back. Roll the dice again, and move your Hero backwards that amount of spaces (if you land on a Hero or Monster you're both destroyed).

5+ Trap fails to go off (you are safe).
If your Hero is a Rogue, the trap is disarmed and you can either CLAIM or KEEP it.

Place a Rogue Marker on the Trap to CLAIM it. Your Heroes do not set off Traps that you've claimed when landed on.

Place the Trap in the Traps Collected area to the left to KEEP it. This gives ALL your Heroes a +1 dice roll bonus when they next land on a Trap (these bonuses stack).

If you claim or keep a trap already claimed by another player, their Rogue Marker is returned to them.

CLASS: MAGE / SKILL: COLLECT POTIONS

SPECIAL ITEMS

Place below when a Mage ends its turn on top of them. Dropped if that Hero is destroyed (by potion effect, Monster, Hero, or Trap).

 SWORD +1 to all combat dice rolls with this Hero

 SHOES This Hero doesn't set off any Traps

 SHIELD A Hero with a shield is knocked back into the nearest free space when an opponent's Hero lands on them.

If a Mage lands on a Potion, either USE it straight away, or KEEP it for ANY of your Heroes on the board to use at the start of a later turn (remove potion after use).

STANDARD RED PLAYER HERO SHEET

POTIONS COLLECTED

Stack potions collected by the Mage here.

LANDING ON A POTION

Potions are removed from the board after use. If a Mage lands on a potion, you can choose to COLLECT it for later use.

1 Teleport. Roll the dice again, and move your Hero forwards that number of spaces (if you land on a Hero, Monster or Potion it is destroyed).

2-3 Death Pulse. Any untamed Monster/other player's Hero in an adjacent square is destroyed and removed from the board (the other player's Hero is returned to the Spawning Portal)

4-5 Switcheroo. Switch places with another player's Hero, or Monster of your choice. If there aren't any Heroes or Monsters in front of you, the opportunity is lost and the potion removed.

6 Flick A Foe. Remove either another player's Hero or a Monster from the board (the Hero is returned to the Spawning Portal).

CLASS: WARRIOR / SKILL: TAME MONSTER

SPECIAL ITEMS

Place below when a Warrior ends its turn on top of them. Dropped if that Hero is destroyed (by potion effect, Monster, Hero, or Trap).

 SWORD +1 to all combat dice rolls with this Hero

 SHOES This Hero doesn't set off any Traps

 SHIELD A Hero with a shield is knocked back into the nearest free space when an opponent's Hero lands on them.

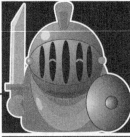

WARRIOR MARKERS

Place Warrior Markers below, for use when TAMING a Monster.

MONSTERS KEPT

+1 per Monster

+1 per Monster

+1 per Monster

+1 per Monster

LANDING ON A MONSTER

1-3 The Monster defeats you.
Place your Hero in the Spawning Portal to await resurrection.

4+ You defeat the Monster. Remove the Monster from the board, unless your Hero is a Warrior.

If your Hero is a Warrior, you can either TAME or KEEP the Monster.

Place a Warrior Marker on the Monster's board square to TAME it. You do not need to roll a dice if ANY of your Heroes land on this Monster.

Place the Monster in the Monsters Kept area to the left to KEEP it. This gives ALL your Heroes a +1 dice roll bonus when they next land on a Monster you haven't Tamed (these bonuses stack).

If you Tame, Keep or Defeat a Monster already Tamed by another player, their Warrior Marker is returned to them.

Traps are reset after they've been triggered, and can only be removed by a Rogue.

If you land on a Trap and your Hero is not carrying the Special Item 'Shoes', roll a dice.

1 Trap Zap. Hero is electrocuted, and returns to the Spawning Portal to await resurrection. ☠

2-4 Fling Back. Roll the dice again, and move your Hero backwards that amount of spaces. If you land on another Hero or Monster then you are both instantly destroyed (Heroes return to the Spawning Portal, and Monsters are removed from the board). If you land on another Trap, then you must make a Trap dice roll again. If you land on a Potion or Special Item, it is destroyed (remove it from the board).

5+ Trap fails to go off (you are safe). If your Hero is a Rogue, the Trap is disarmed and you can either CLAIM or KEEP it.

TO CLAIM IT: Place a Rogue Marker from your Rogue's Hero Sheet on the Trap. Your Heroes do not set off Traps that you've claimed when landed on.

TO KEEP IT: Place the Trap in the Traps Collected area of your Rogue's Hero Sheet. This gives ALL your Heroes a +1 dice roll bonus when they next land on a trap (These bonuses stack. Collect 3 traps and you get +3).

If you Claim or Keep a Trap already Claimed by another player, return their Rogue Marker.

Potions are removed from the board after use. If a Mage lands on a potion, the Mage can choose to collect it for later instead of using it now (see Collected Potions below).

If you land on a Potion, or are using a potion your Mage collected earlier, roll a dice.

1 Teleport. Roll the dice again, and move your Hero forwards that number of spaces. If you land on another Hero, Monster or Potion then it is destroyed and returned to the Spawning Portal/removed from the board (your own Hero is unaffected). If you land on a Trap, it fails to trigger (you can CLAIM or KEEP it, if your Hero is a Rogue). If you land on a Special Item, it is collected.

2-3 Death Pulse. Any Monster/other player's Hero in an adjacent square is destroyed and removed from the board (the other player's Hero is returned to the Spawning Portal).

4-5 Switcheroo. Switch places with another player's Hero, or Monster of your choice. If there aren't any Heroes or Monsters in front of you, the opportunity is lost and the potion removed.

6 Flick A Foe. Remove either another player's Hero or a Monster from the board (the Hero is returned to the Spawning Portal).

COLLECTED POTIONS

If a Mage has collected a potion, it can be used by ANY of that player's Heroes on the board at the start of that player's turn, before moving (Only 1 potion may be used at a time). After use, the potion is discarded.

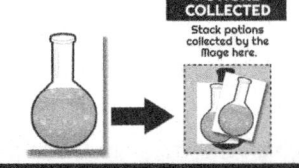

Monsters only attack when a Hero lands on their square. The Warrior is the only Hero that can TAME or KEEP Monsters.

If you land on a Monster that you haven't TAMED (see below), roll a dice. Add 1 to the dice roll for every Monster your Warrior has KEPT (see below). If your Hero has the 'Sword' Special Item add 1.

1-3 The Monster defeats you. Place your Hero in the Spawning Portal to await resurrection. ☠

4+ You defeat the Monster. Remove the Monster from the board, unless your Hero is a Warrior. If your Hero is a Warrior, you can either TAME or KEEP the Monster.

TO TAME IT: Place a Warrior Marker from your Warrior's Hero Sheet on the same board square as the Monster. Your Heroes do not get attacked by Monsters you've Tamed.

TO KEEP IT: Place the Monster in the Monsters Kept area of your Warrior's Hero Sheet. This gives ALL your Heroes a +1 dice roll bonus when they land on a Monster (these bonuses stack. Collect 3 Monsters and you get +3).

If you Tame, Keep or Defeat a Monster already Tamed by another player, return their Warrior Marker.

Special Items grant powerful bonuses to the Hero that collects them, and are dropped if that Hero is destroyed (by potion effect, monster, opponent's Hero, or trap).

If the Special Items have been placed in a stack (rather than individually), the Hero that lands on the stack may choose which item to take.

There are 3 Special Items to collect: Sword, Shoes, and Shield. When collected, the Special Item is placed in the Special Items area of that Hero's Character Sheet.

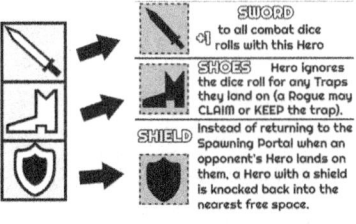

 SWORD +1 to all combat dice rolls with this Hero

 SHOE This Hero ignores the dice roll for any traps they land on (if the Hero is a Rogue, they may CLAIM or KEEP the trap).

 SHIELD Instead of returning to the Spawning Portal when an opponent's Hero lands on them, a Hero with a shield is knocked back into the nearest free space (no points are gained from landing on a Hero who's carrying a Shield).

Once you're a bit more familiar with the game, try turning the Hero Sheets over to their 'Advanced' side for an extra challenge. On the right side you'll find each individual Hero has a Sub Class which includes a Special Skill that can be used under certain conditions.

BARBARIAN	WITCH	THIEF	WIZARD	KNIGHT	ASSASSIN	NECROMANCER	VALKYRIE	TRICKSTER

BERSERK	CURSE	STEAL	CURE	SECOND WIND	BACKSTAB	RESURRECT	OPERA BLAST	SPEED BURST

On the other side of Board A you'll find the alternative Board B. This board has two unconnected boards (one on the left side, and one on the right), each with their own Spawning Portal. It's best used for low conflict two player games, with one player spawning on the left side and one on the right. It's still possible for players to 'invade' each others board side using the 'Switcheroo' potion power, though mostly you'll be trying to race each other to the exit.

♦ You can also use just one side of Board B, with both players spawning in the same portal, for quick games.

When setting up Board B:

♦ Monsters, Traps and Potions should be distributed evenly between the two board sides.

♦ Place the Special Item 'Shoes' in the middle of one board side, and the Special Item 'Sword' in the middle of the other (assigned at random). The Special Item 'Shield' is removed from play, as there's less chance you'll be landing on the other player's Heroes.

There's a range of FREE Board Horde resources to download at **www.davidhailwood.com**. This includes full colour boards, Hero Sheets, 3D printable materials and more!

  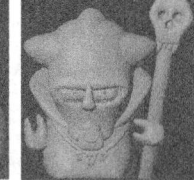

CUT OUT THE FOLLOWING HERO SHEET PAGES, BOARDS AND SCOREBOARD TO USE IN THE GAME!

CLASS: ROGUE / SKILL: DISARM TRAPS

SPECIAL ITEMS

Place below when a Rogue ends its turn on top of them. Dropped if that Hero is destroyed (by potion effect, Monster, Hero, or Trap).

 **SWORD** +1 to all combat dice rolls with this Hero

SHOES Hero doesn't set off Traps (a Rogue may CLAIM or KEEP the trap).

SHIELD A Hero with a shield is knocked back into the nearest free space when an opponent's Hero lands on them.

ROGUE MARKERS

Place Rogue Markers below, for use when CLAIMING a Trap.

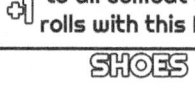

TRAPS COLLECTED

+1 per Trap

If a Rogue avoids setting off a Trap, either CLAIM it, or KEEP it above.

If ANY of your Heroes (not just the Rogue) land on a Trap, add 1 to the dice roll for each Trap stacked here.

LANDING ON A TRAP 🎲

1 Trap Zap. Hero returns to the Spawning Portal to await resurrection.

2-4 Fling Back. Roll the dice again, and move your Hero backwards that amount of spaces (if you land on a Hero or Monster you're both destroyed).

5+ Trap fails to go off (you are safe). If your Hero is a Rogue, the trap is disarmed and you can either CLAIM or KEEP it.

Place a Rogue Marker on the Trap to CLAIM it. Your Heroes do not set off Traps that you've claimed when landed on.

Place the Trap in the Traps Collected area to the left to KEEP it. This gives ALL your Heroes a +1 dice roll bonus when they next land on a Trap (these bonuses stack).

If you claim or keep a trap already claimed by another player, their Rogue Marker is returned to them.

CLASS: MAGE / SKILL: COLLECT POTIONS

SPECIAL ITEMS

Place below when a Mage ends its turn on top of them. Dropped if that Hero is destroyed (by potion effect, Monster, Hero, or Trap).

SWORD +1 to all combat dice rolls with this Hero

SHOES This Hero doesn't set off any Traps

SHIELD A Hero with a shield is knocked back into the nearest free space when an opponent's Hero lands on them.

If a Mage lands on a Potion, either USE it straight away, or KEEP it for ANY of your Heroes on the board to use at the start of a later turn (remove potion after use).

STANDARD BLUE PLAYER HERO SHEET

POTIONS COLLECTED

Stack potions collected by the Mage here.

LANDING ON A POTION 🎲

Potions are removed from the board after use. If a Mage lands on a potion, you can choose to COLLECT it for later use.

1 Teleport. Roll the dice again, and move your Hero forwards that number of spaces (if you land on a Hero, Monster or Potion it is destroyed).

2-3 Death Pulse. Any untamed Monster/other player's Hero in an adjacent square is destroyed and removed from the board (the other player's Hero is returned to the Spawning Portal)

4-5 Switcheroo. Switch places with another player's Hero, or Monster of your choice. If there aren't any Heroes or Monsters in front of you, the opportunity is lost and the potion removed.

6 Flick A Foe. Remove either another player's Hero or a Monster from the board (the Hero is returned to the Spawning Portal).

CLASS: WARRIOR / SKILL: TAME MONSTER

SPECIAL ITEMS

Place below when a Warrior ends its turn on top of them. Dropped if that Hero is destroyed (by potion effect, Monster, Hero, or Trap).

SWORD +1 to all combat dice rolls with this Hero

SHOES This Hero doesn't set off any Traps

SHIELD A Hero with a shield is knocked back into the nearest free space when an opponent's Hero lands on them.

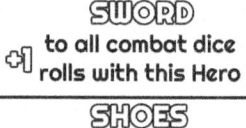

WARRIOR MARKERS

Place Warrior Markers below, for use when TAMING a Monster.

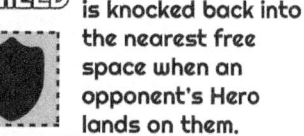

MONSTERS KEPT

+1 per Monster

+1 per Monster

+1 per Monster

+1 per Monster

LANDING ON A MONSTER 🎲

1-3 The Monster defeats you. Place your Hero in the Spawning Portal to await resurrection.

4+ You defeat the Monster. Remove the Monster from the board, unless your Hero is a Warrior.

If your Hero is a Warrior, you can either TAME or KEEP the Monster.

Place a Warrior Marker on the Monster's board square to TAME it. You do not need to roll a dice if ANY of your Heroes land on this Monster.

Place the Monster in the Monsters Kept area to the left to KEEP it. This gives ALL your Heroes a +1 dice roll bonus when they next land on a Monster you haven't Tamed (these bonuses stack).

If you Tame, Keep or Defeat a Monster already Tamed by another player, their Warrior Marker is returned to them.

CLASS: ROGUE / SKILL: DISARM TRAPS

SPECIAL ITEMS

Place below when a Rogue ends its turn on top of them. Dropped if that Hero is destroyed (by potion effect, Monster, Hero, or Trap).

 **SWORD** +1 to all combat dice rolls with this Hero

 **SHOES** Hero doesn't set off Traps (a Rogue may CLAIM or KEEP the trap).

 **SHIELD** A Hero with a shield is knocked back into the nearest free space when an opponent's Hero lands on them.

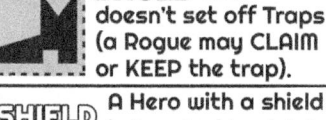

ROGUE MARKERS

Place Rogue Markers below, for use when CLAIMING a Trap.

TRAPS COLLECTED

+1 per Trap

If a Rogue avoids setting off a Trap, either CLAIM it, or KEEP it above.

If ANY of your Heroes (not just the Rogue) land on a Trap, add 1 to the dice roll for each Trap stacked here.

SUBCLASS: THIEF
SPECIAL SKILL: LIGHT FINGERED

If the Thief ends its turn on a square behind a Special Item, or behind an opponent's Hero who's carrying a Special Item, the Thief steals it for itself.

CLASS: MAGE / SKILL: COLLECT POTIONS

SPECIAL ITEMS

Place below when a Mage ends its turn on top of them. Dropped if that Hero is destroyed (by potion effect, Monster, Hero, or Trap).

 **SWORD** +1 to all combat dice rolls with this Hero

 **SHOES** This Hero doesn't set off any Traps

 **SHIELD** A Hero with a shield is knocked back into the nearest free space when an opponent's Hero lands on them.

POTIONS COLLECTED

Stack potions collected by the Mage here.

If a Mage lands on a Potion, either USE it straight away, or KEEP it for ANY of your Heroes on the board to use at the start of a later turn (remove potion after use).

ADVANCED BLUE PLAYER HERO SHEET

SUBCLASS: WITCH
SPECIAL SKILL: CURSE

If the Witch ends her turn on a square behind an opponent's Hero, she puts a Curse on them. Roll a dice and move their Hero backwards by the amount of spaces shown on the dice (if the space is occupied, move the Hero to a free space closest to the number on the dice).

CLASS: WARRIOR / SKILL: TAME MONSTER

SPECIAL ITEMS

Place below when a Warrior ends its turn on top of them. Dropped if that Hero is destroyed (by potion effect, Monster, Hero, or Trap).

 **SWORD** +1 to all combat dice rolls with this Hero

 **SHOES** This Hero doesn't set off any Traps

SHIELD A Hero with a shield is knocked back into the nearest free space when an opponent's Hero lands on them.

WARRIOR MARKERS

Place Warrior Markers below, for use when TAMING a Monster.

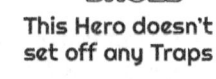
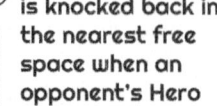

MONSTERS KEPT

+1 per Monster

+1 per Monster

+1 per Monster

+1 per Monster

SUBCLASS: BARBARIAN
SPECIAL SKILL: BERSERK

If the Barbarian ends his turn on a square between two Monsters (except ones he's tamed), two opposing Heroes, or a Monster and an opposing Hero, he knocks both off the board (Heroes are returned to the Spawning Portal)

BOARD HORDE

BOARD **B** LEFT SIDE

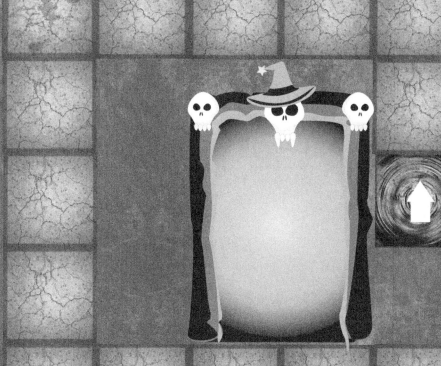

LANDING ON A TRAP:
1 Trap Zap
2-4 Fling Back ←
5+ Trap fails to go off

LANDING ON
A MONSTER:
1-3 Hero
4+ Monster

BOARD HORDE · **BOARD A** LEFT SIDE

LANDING ON A TRAP: 🎲🎲
1 Trap Zap 💀
2-4 Fling Back 🎲 ⬅
5+ Trap fails to go off

LANDING ON A MONSTER: 🎲🎲
1-3 Hero 💀
4+ Monster 💀

BOARD HORDE

BOARD A RIGHT SIDE

LANDING ON A POTION:
1 Teleport ➡
2-3 Death Pulse

4-5 Switcheroo
6 Flick A Foe

BOARD HORDE

BOARD B RIGHT SIDE

LANDING ON A POTION:

1 Teleport

2-3 Death Pulse

4-5 Switcheroo

6 Flick A Foe

23
22 21 20 19 18 17 16 15 14
24 25 26 27 28 29 30 13
31 12
38 37 36 35 34 33 32 11
39
40 41 42 43 44 10
49 48 47 46 45 9
0 1 2 3 4 5 6 7 8

SCORING:

HERO DEFEATED 3 Pts
EXIT REACHED 10 Pts
POTION COLLECTED 1 Pt
SPECIAL ITEM COLLECTED 1 Pt
MONSTER DEFEATED/
CLAIMED/TAMED 3 Pts
TRAP AVOIDED/
CLAIMED/COLLECTED 3 Pts

Printed in Great Britain
by Amazon

32097060R00064